LES

EXPANDING RESPONSE JOURNALS

IN ALL SUBJECT AREAS

HEINEMANN
Portsmouth, NH

© 1994 Pembroke Publishers Limited
538 Hood Road
Markham, Ontario L3R 3K9

Canadian Cataloguing in Publication Data
Parsons, Less, 1943-
 Expanding response journals — in any subject area

Includes bibliographical references and index.
ISBN 1-55138-022-6

1. School children – Diaries. 2. Creative writing
(Elementary education). 3. Reading (Elementary) –
Language experience approach. 4. Language arts –
Correlation with content subjects. I. Title.

LB1576.P37 1994   372.6'23   C94-930143-4

Published in the U.S.A. by Heinemann
A Division of Reed Publishing (USA) Inc.
361 Hanover Street
Portsmouth, NH 03801-3912

Library of Congress Cataloging-in-Publication Data
Parsons, Les.
 Expanding response journals II : Integrating the curriculum /
Les Parsons
 p.   cm.
 Includes bibliographical references and index.
 ISBN 0-435-08813-0
 1. Language arts (Elementary) 2. Reading (Elementary)–Language
experience approach. 3. Written communication–Study and teaching.
(Elementary). I. Title. II. Title: Expanding response journals 2.
III. Title: Expanding response journals two.
 LB1576.P262   1993
 372.6—dc20   93-47193
                                                    CIP

Editor: David Kilgour
Cover design by John Zehethofer
Cover photography by Ajay Photographics
Typesetting by Jay Tee Graphics Ltd.

Printed and bound in Canada
9 8 7 6 5 4 3 2 1

Contents

Foreword

Many teachers now use response journals in their English programs. As the strategy has become more widely known, however, teachers across the curriculum have begun to appreciate how essential personal response is to learning in all subject areas. *Expanding Response Journals* is meant for those teachers, opening up the entire process of using response journals to everyone.

I designed the book to be a practical, hands-on guide; novice and experienced teachers alike should find their questions about how and why to use response journals fully answered. Sample student responses from every area of the curriculum are used throughout the book to demonstrate how effectively personal response can assist and enhance learning.

Expanding Response Journals also recognizes the expertise and teaching style of the individual teacher. Once teachers gain confidence with the basic techniques of personal response, they can begin to tailor the use of journals to their own needs and those of their students. This book serves as a starting point — the possibilities that flow from personal response are endless.

1 * Responding across the curriculum

Facing the learning reality

In any classroom, regardless of subject area, and at any given time, students are trying to make sense out of what's going on to determine what relevance, if any, it all has with their own personal lives. Since each student is centred in a different subjective context, each one finds the experience colored in a different way. One student was up late last night, alone, watching television, just as he has been all week, another student had a bitter fight with her boyfriend just before class began, and another slept in this morning, missed breakfast, and, as usual, got to school late. In various similar but profoundly different ways, each student in the class begins the classroom learning experience with a separate set of priorities stemming from a separate, personal point of view.

The teacher, unaware of all that has happened to these students since last they met, even in other classrooms, begins to talk about recreation in the nineteenth century, mentioning that the game of curling was played outside on frozen rivers. Immediately, another set of experiential factors are wrapped around the lesson to further confound and blunt the intended learning experience. Between the three students who have never heard of curling and the two students who curl every weekend is a gamut of shifting and conflicting, vicarious, real, and imagined experiences and an accompanying range of interests, attitudes, and values.

Imagine, as well, how a film on mid-western farming may be received. As the images unfold, one student begins thinking about the trip out west she and her family took two years ago, how hot it was in the car, and how often her parents fought. Another thinks it looks really boring compared to the city, but it doesn't really matter because it's just a prelude to whatever work he'll have to do after the film is over. Just tell him what to do and he'll do it. Still another begins to daydream, caught up in the vivid images of golden grain, blue sky, and distant horizons, while one forlorn individual, reliving an emotional conflict of a few minutes ago, still dabs at tears.

Teachers can view these cluttered, complex, and compelling facts of classroom life either as the source of resistance to and interference with the experience of learning or as the stuff of which learning is made. They can ignore or discount these states of mind and these experiences or capitalize on them. They can attend to brain research and help students make the connections and discover the patterns that reveal meaning and produce insight, or they can fill their hours with rote memorization and copying of notes.

To become life-long learners, students need to be persuaded that the search for meaning begins with their own feelings, attitudes, and values. They need to chart and explore what they've been through and use those beginnings as their personal springboards into a study of the world around them. For an ESL (English as a Second Language) student, the learning may begin with a series of questions:

What is this curling?
Where is there a picture?
How do you play it?
How many people do this?

For others, the beginning may be a detailed description of last weekend's curling match or a western vacation two years ago, an emotional defence of life in the city, or a poem celebrating the beauty of the natural world. For at least one student, no other learning will take place that day until she learns how to sort out her inner turmoil. But in every classroom, regardless of subject area, and at any given time, the diverse and fragmented learning/teaching environment can be ultimately resolved and integrated through a learning/teaching strategy called personal response.

Journals, journals everywhere

Throughout the educational community, the use of response journals has spread quickly and widely. From primary classrooms to adult education, most teachers, by this time, have experimented with some form of journal-keeping. As with any popular innovation, however, questions continue to spring up about the "nuts and bolts" of using response journals, as well as how wide-spread that use should be.

While many teachers have discovered that response journals help satisfy a major portion of their learning/teaching objectives, others have expressed genuine concerns. They wonder whether the technique can be adapted to specialized curricula, the specific needs of their students, or even the nature of their own idiosyncratic teaching styles. Since response journals have found their way mainly into English and language arts classrooms, the foremost question from teachers in other subject areas is, "What do response journals have to do with me?" If those teachers are looking for ways to enhance, deepen, and integrate learning across the curriculum, the answer is, "Everything."

Rave reviews

Before examining why the use of response journals should be expanded across the curriculum and the mechanics of how to accomplish that goal, we need to address the way in which journals are presently being employed in classrooms. Ideally, personal responses act first as a mirror, enabling individuals to recognize what they are thinking and the patterns created by that process; in the subsequent, reflective stage, the responses then form a window into the very nature of these thoughts, establishing how and why individuals actually learn.

As a case in point, a thirteen-year-old, barely two years out of ESL (English as a Second Language) classes, wrote an unsolicited poem to express and define what her response journal meant to her. Once integrated into regular classes and introduced to response journals, she immediately discovered that personal response allowed her to take control of her own learning.

When she recognized how essential the technique had become to her own well-being as a learner, she began to examine the theme in poetic form. The theme was so important to her that she returned to this poem over the course of a year, revising it significantly time and again to suit the ever-widening vision she was gaining of her own learning processes. Notice how intrinsically her confidence and sense of self-worth are tied to the process of response and reflection, even in the use of the appropriate personal pronoun. She clearly demonstrates that she is a capable, self-motivated thinker who knows how she learns.

Response to journal-keeping

This one is for one of my teachers.
She taught me how to express myself.
I can tell her things by heart
And she understands what I feel.

I can learn things by seeing her face.
Her brain remembers every word I say,
Every dot, every letter.
She whispers into my ears.
If something is good, she talks smoothly.

She taught me how to sing high, sing low.
She guides me.
Whether I'm happy or sad, I'll still talk to her.
I share my adventures all the time.
She shows me why I do things.
She teaches me every day.

She cares about me,
She loves me,
She knows how to read my mind.
You can only find her by your imagination.
I'll love her forever... my response journal.

Evelyn Y. (age 13)

Mixed reviews

On the other hand, the popularity of journal use has been a mixed blessing. Current curriculum writers feel compelled to add journal-writing as a prominent learning/teaching strategy in curriculum guides ranging from family studies to mathematics. While the use of response journals is extolled, unfortunately, the superficial and brief manner in which the topic is usually handled in these documents only adds to the confusion and misunderstanding that have always surrounded journals. Consequently, many teachers tend to include journal-writing in their programs out of a sense of obligation rather than from a belief in its value.

The practice of journal-writing is still often approached as a kind of enforced diary-keeping, detached and separate from the real content of classroom programs and excluded from the evaluation systems that drive them. The results of such an approach can be perfunctory and ultimately of little or no use in the learning process.

Is it any wonder that we still hear students say...

"I did journals in grade four. Why are we doing 'baby' stuff?"

"Journals are boring!"

"When are we going to do real work?"

"What should I write about?"

"We did this in English class. Why are we doing it again?"

"Does this count on the report card?"

Is it any wonder that teachers ask...

"What do you do when students get tired of writing in their journals?"

"I teach in a school with a rotary timetable. If students kept journals in every subject, wouldn't it get boring?"

"How can I be expected to spend time on journals, when I have to evaluate my students' learning?"

"What should students write in their journals? How much time should I spend on them?"

"In what subject areas should journals be used? What good are they, really?"

"What about students with learning difficulties? Should they use journals?"

Keeping journals for the sake of keeping journals or because a curriculum guide says your students should keep journals is pointless and counter-productive. A fresh examination of response journals is essential before their potential as a multi-dimensional, learning/teaching tool can be realized.

What is a response journal?

A response journal is a notebook or folder in which students record, in a variety of formats, their personal reactions to, questions about, and reflections on:

• what they read, write, observe, listen to, discuss, do, and think ("doing" includes such activities as making, performing, calculating, experimenting, manipulating, or creating);

• how they actually go about reading, writing, observing, listening, discussing, or doing.

As such, the journal may be a separate notebook or a section in a notebook in a particular subject area. In a rotary timetable, a group of teachers could share a notebook or a personal response section of a binder, in effect creating an independent study theme across a number of subject areas. On the other hand, a science notebook could have a separate personal response section devoted solely to that subject. Whatever the arrangement, the only restriction is that students must be aware of the personal response process and must have some kind of recording routine to accommodate both the process and the evaluation of that process.

In some cases a journal entry might comprise the entire follow-up to a lesson; in others, the teacher might allot a few minutes at the end of a period to check on students' reactions and make suggestions for other possible reading or projects. Either way, response journal entries provide an invaluable barometer of students' feelings and learning.

A response journal is...

• a convenient, familiar, and flexible method for students to record, explore, and reflect on their personal responses to such diverse learning experiences as

    — a science experiment
    — a field trip
    — using a blow-torch in a metal shop
    — a mathematics lesson
    — a small-group discussion in family studies
    — writing-in-role in a history class
    — viewing a film or television program

• a technique to ensure that higher-level thinking processes are regularly addressed and that learning is routinely personalized, deepened, and extended

• a way for learning to be integrated and evaluated across the curriculum

• a place for students to record their individual perspectives on small- and large-group discussions and their roles in the discussion dynamics of the group

• a reference file to help both student and teacher monitor individual development and progress for both formative and summative evaluation purposes

• another way for individual students to "dialogue" in written form with their teachers and peers

Personal response and learning

Learning is an active, creative process. Most definitions of ideal learners emphasize that they are independent, self-motivated individuals who have the ability to find and solve their own problems. This kind of empowerment can come only through the acquisition of a complex set of sophisticated, metacognitive skills. By definition, such learners are profoundly aware of their own learning processes.

The term "whole learning" recognizes that language and learning are intrinsically linked. Learning may, at any one time, incorporate some or all aspects of language. By the same token, the act of processing language involves more than the communicating or recording of experience. Through language, we construct our sense of reality by revealing, clarifying, discovering, assessing, reflecting on, and refining what we think and feel about our experiences.

The learning process combines elements of reading, writing, listening, speaking, observing, doing, and thinking. Through the use of response journals, students can reflect not only on what they've been learning but also on how and why they learn the way they do. Through a personal response program, they are able to develop the awareness of and, eventually, the commitment to the kind of processes necessary to facilitate and maximize their learning.

Throughout this book, sample responses provide a concrete idea of what a response journal looks like when some of these learning objectives are translated into positive student outcomes. These sometimes abbreviated excerpts offer a glimpse into the variety of possible responses and the many functions served by response journals. Spelling errors have been corrected, but other stylistic features remain as they appeared in the originals.

Sample integrated response

The brain naturally integrates (See *Responding to brain research*, page 19). In its search for connections, it jumps spontaneously from thought to thought and from concept to concept, regardless of barriers such as the designated subject areas found in most schools. To the brain, and to students, those barriers don't actually exist.

In a fused history-geography course, for example, a young student assumed the identity of a nineteenth-century North American aboriginal leader named Chief Seattle. After reading one of his speeches in a picture-book, *Brother Eagle, Sister Moon*, she chose to write in role, giving his reactions to the contemporary world. In her response journal afterwards, she discussed her feelings about the central issues. For this student, the divisions separating the subjects of history, geography, English, and science were non-existent. Her need to make sense of an issue automatically eliminated subject-specific barriers.

When I began to think like Chief Seattle, I got angry and sad, all at the same time. If we had taken what Chief Seattle had said seriously, then we might not have these terrible environmental problems now. It's time that we take a stand before we let the earth rot away. Chief Seattle was a wise man. He could see what was going to happen to the future. Even if we don't know what the future will bring, we can use the three "R's" (recycle, reduce, reuse). We need to cut down trees more wisely and try to stop putting chemicals that pollute into the air and we might be able to help. Chief Seattle spoke about his children and the children to come. We have to do this for ourselves, for our children and our children's children, and hope they'll take care of the earth better than we have.

Yvonne L. (age 12)

Have your students "metacognated" lately?

Whenever learning theories are discussed, the term "metacognition" inevitably surfaces. One of the differences between educational theorists and educational practitioners is their jargon. Practitioners, for the most part, are often repelled by jargon theorists find invaluable. "Metacognition" is a case in point. Many practitioners find the term confusing and even pretentious. Nevertheless, the concept is crucial to an understanding of learning and how learning can be facilitated through personal response.

Metacognition refers to the ability to consciously reflect on and talk about thinking; specifically, learners begin to focus on their patterns of thought and become aware of how and, eventually, why they process experiences the specific way they do. This ability is enhanced by developmental factors and encouraged by reflective practices, such as personal response. Although students can engage in higher-level thinking processes without it, independent, self-motivated learners require metacognitive ability to reach their goals.

Thinking is a process

How is metacognition different from other processes requiring higher-level thinking? Actually, the processes are the same; only the focus is changed. Take these sample processes that require higher-level thinking:

- defining problems
- formulating questions
- generating hypotheses
- drawing conclusions
- selecting criteria in order to make assessments
- justifying points of view

Assume that a student gets an incorrect answer for a word problem in math. He or she decides that the fault must lie either in the mechanics of the calculations or in the reading of the original problem. The student investigates, discovers the error, corrects it, and gets the right answer. The student has been engaged in higher-level thinking processes. Metacognition, on the other hand, requires that the focus for these processes be the student's own actual thought patterns, as in the next example.

Sample responses to a metacognitive process

In the following response, these processes can be identified or inferred as the student traces how he came to a key learning breakthrough. Central to this seemingly simple triumph is the realization that his interior emotional life is both a positive, creative force and a hindrance to his learning. While, to an outsider, the choice of pen is an obvious solution to an obvious problem, from the learner's perspective, the problem and solution were opaque over a long period of time. On the other hand, the complex insight into his emotional responses is offered in almost an off-hand manner.

Response to visual arts

I learned one key thing. It doesn't take much time to become good at art. You don't have to be a genius. All it takes is a pen, pencil, some colors, and a lot of creativity. At the beginning of the year, I didn't know what to do in art. I basically just couldn't concentrate long enough. But then one day in January, I finally figured out the secret to doing art. I was trying too hard! Everyone else was relaxed. I mean, I'm just hacking away at my art and everyone else is calm and relaxed.

The second step in being a good artist is a good pen. You see, when I got this pen, it was a micro-fine tip pen. So, I was using the micro-fine and wondering why my lines and dots weren't as thick and dark as the other people's in the room. I was frustrated, really frustrated. I was so frustrated that I was about to tear up my work. Then I found out I was using the wrong kind of pen.

Last of all, you need creativity to be an artist. I remember when I was doing my mood art at the beginning of the year. I furiously colored my art and then I tore it up. That was my art for angry.

Po Wang N. (age 14)

The most straightforward type of metacognitive reflection involves taking stock of where you are now, where you've come from, and analyzing what has happened to produce the discovered growth or change in your performance. Since children and adolescents are inherently egocentric, developing this kind of objectivity can be difficult. The process may be tentative and recursive, but awareness gradually takes shape.

In this next sample, the student is able to pull back and almost disinterestedly itemize specific areas of growth, attribute causes, and even assess success. On the other hand, by attaining this perspective on her cognitive development, unlike the previous example, the student has excised or ignored her emotional connections with the learning process. Her analysis is almost disturbingly dispassionate and clinical.

Response to English

> I find I've been doing much more reading than I ever have before. I've found a type of book that I can relate to and enjoy reading and can understand. My vocabulary has broadened from the amount of reading I've been doing.
>
> Most of what I've been reading has been young adult novels. Although I enjoy reading now, I like to stick to mystery or romance books. I have finally taken the step of being able to comprehend the language being used. I think this may be helping my writing as well.
>
> Leanne S. (age 14)

In the final sample, the student displays considerable self-awareness, passion, and insight. In a guidance class, after a period of small-group discussion based on the question, "What should students learn how to do to be successful?" the students were asked to personalize the question by writing in their response journals about their own most memorable or important learning experience.

Most students in the class wrote about work and study habits, a specific subject-related skill, or a subject area in which they had noticed significant improvement. This student refused to be drawn into a discussion of school-related issues. Her own learning transcended success in school or even the most sacred of adolescent goals, popularity and friendship. In the following response, metacognition and the image of an independent, self-motivated learner merge.

The response ends with a bold, ringing, almost defiant, personal affirmation.

Response to guidance

> *I've learned to make my own choices through experience (the best way!). That's memorable because I still do make my own choices and important because you won't always have someone there and you're going to have to make your own choices soon enough. What then? You won't know what to do. Plus, if you let someone else make all your choices for you, you're going to end up doing things you don't want to or don't like. The effect is that I'm independent and strong and if I lose friends, I won't die!*
>
> *Jen R. (age 13)*

Responding to brain research

Some educators point to brain research to support their claims that certain students are physiologically limited in how they process experience. They suggest, for example, that affective, cognitive, and psychomotor processes are distinct and separate entities and that, consequently, each requires distinct and separate instruction. Educational behaviorists have long insisted that rote memorization is the brain's preferred mode of learning, while many educators also accept as proven that people have preferred or dominant left- or right-brain processing tendencies. In fact, the language of "hemisphericity" (or right- and left-brain processes) has become a fixture of educational jargon. As a case in point, some educators theorize that, since the left brain controls speech and most language functions and the right brain controls visual spatial skills, by diagnosing a child's tendencies toward right- or left-brain use, teachers can teach to the favored hemisphere with greater success.

Educators may be making these claims, but not brain researchers.

Recent research has even brought into question the centuries-old belief that movement on one side of the body is controlled by the half of the brain on the opposite side. Researchers unexpectedly discovered that, regardless of whether someone is left- or right-handed, the left hemisphere is important for movement of *both* left and right hands. The right hemisphere is important for the movement of *only* the left hand. The brain clearly functions in a far more complex and integrated manner than many educators would prefer.

Moreover, since much of their previous research data has, necessarily, been taken from situations in which brains have been damaged, researchers are extremely cautious about generalizing their findings to the general population. In cases in which the link between the brain's hemispheres has been severed, the source for educators' claims about hemisphericity, they are especially cautious. Since a healthy brain is an interconnected whole in which both hemispheres simultaneously assist in processing information, the most that can be gleaned and hypothesized from such research is how a brain functions when the sharing of information is impossible. Caine and Caine assert in their book, *Making Connections: Teaching and the Human Brain*, that intuition, holistic images, and synthesis over time — supposedly right-hemispheric functions — can, in fact, be accomplished by anyone, including people whose right hemispheres are dysfunctional. In the same way, educators who claim that the brain is a muscle to be trained and use this as justification for rote memorization or pre-packaged, sequential, programmed learning are ignoring the research affirming that all learners flourish in a rich, varied, and stimulating holistic environment.

Added to this complexity is the key role that emotions play in learning. While educators have long accepted the axiom that affective and cognitive behaviors are two sides of the same coin, they need to recognize the inseparable and interdependent nature of that relationship. To strip content of its emotional connotations and denotations would actually distort and impede learning. Indeed, it's been suggested that emotions are instrumental in shaping our understanding of reality.

Sample response to an emotional experience

Personal responses often have a predictable progression. As in the following sample, they dwell first on the immediate stimulus, move on to related personal experiences, and then open the discussion to probe unresolved issues or to generalize from the issue in question. The teacher had read aloud to the class a story called "The Haunted Graveyard" and the student reacted to it in her response journal. The content, however, is far from predictable. Issues such as hemisphericity and rote learning fade in the vivid, immediate context of real-life learning. Imagine, as well, how impossible it would be to separate the emotional and the intellectual in this response.

Response to a readaloud

In this story, the sound effects impressed me. When the storyteller was scared, she started to cry. It made me nervous and scared too. I'd like to know if the storyteller was the real person in the story. The story reminded me of my first Hallowe'en when I came to this country, so it made it more exciting for me!

But, in truth, are there really ghosts? My grandmother says, "yes," and my father says, "no". That makes it a big question for me. What do you think? And if there was truly a ghost in front of you, what would you do immediately? Would you think fast or run away?

Evelyn H. (age 13)

Through personal response, students trace the course of their learning experiences and, in the process, illuminate that learning both for themselves and for the teacher. As the teacher attempts to gather data for diagnostic, formative, or summative evaluation purposes, such information is clearly invaluable. Imagine the impact of these kinds of revelations, as well, near the beginning of the year when student and teacher are just beginning to get to know each other.

In the following response, the student informs a new teacher of a change in her attitude toward and success with problem-solving. Her insights into her own learning are specific and comprehensive. As is so often evident in personal response, shifts in cognitive and affective behaviours are intertwined. In this case, the student has bolstered her confidence to the extent that she is now delighted to learn from her mistakes.

Response to mathematics (problem-solving)

Although we have only been back to school for a short time, I've developed a new skill in math. Last year, I hated mental math or problem-solving, but this year I love "stumpers" because I finally learned how to do it.

At the beginning of each period, Mrs. F. puts up a tricky, exciting "stumper" on the board. We must solve the problem by the end of the period or we are declared stumped. Several times, I got the right answer to the question and I felt great satisfaction. It just makes me feel good and, sometimes, even though I have an incorrect answer, I still feel delighted because I tried!

Now I know that I hated problem-solving so much last year simply because I didn't know how to think logically. But now my mind has learned how to think carefully, step by step, using only the information that is necessary. And then, after I have figured out the answer, I look at it and ask myself one question. Does the answer make sense? This is just one easy, simple method to guide you when solving a problem. I'm just so anxious and can't wait to learn more this year!

Vivian V. (age 11)

Since events in the distant past are so removed by time and experience from students' immediate lives, making history meaningful remains a distinct and continuing challenge. Many teachers use simulation exercises based on historical episodes to create vicarious experiences. These role-playing exercises allow students to respond emotionally and with increasing insight into values and processes far removed from their actual lives. By adding a personal response component, these experiences can be deepened and extended in significant ways.

The two techniques are highlighted in the following student response to a simulation exercise. In small groups, the students had completed a barter simulation in which groups of North American aboriginal people and early European settlers attempted to trade with each other. The trade goods were represented on cards. One of the problems encountered by the students was determining the relative value of trading items; their understanding of value was necessarily prejudiced by their contemporary existence. What is knowing how to survive the winter worth, for example, when compared to a gun or iron pot? After the exercise, when the value of trade items from a seventeenth-century perspective was revealed, the students were visibly frustrated. In their view, the rules had been changed after the fact. In a small way, they had experienced a form of culture shock.

In her subsequent journal entry, this student attempted to explore what significance this simulation exercise might have in a real-life context. As she reflects on the experience, she begins to clarify how and why her ideas have developed. Her conclusions reveal a surprisingly stark and vivid picture of life as it might have been.

Response to a simulation exercise (historical theme)

In real life, both sides would have known about this stuff a lot better than we did. It would have been harder to trade things for a good bargain because the more times you traded, the more you would learn about what things were worth. The more you learned what the other side was trying to do, you should start to ask yourself, "Do I really need this?"

But anyhow, no matter if it is the game or in real life, I still think the native people had the advantage in trading at the beginning. They lived there and they knew what the country and the weather were like and they knew what it was like in some awful situation and how to survive through it. For example, winter is really hard to survive, especially when the Europeans came to this strange, unknown world with absolutely no thoughts about how cold and stormy it would be. Without any preparation, of course it is going to be hard. The rivers might be frozen and they might not be able to move their ships and if they really could, it would be so snowy and stormy, they would have nowhere to go. They would be stuck in the middle of winter with their food running out. People would be getting scurvy. What could they do?

So the natives had absolutely a full advantage of the trading because they knew how to survive. I'd like to know why they didn't just get everything from the Europeans so long as the Europeans wanted to stay alive. The Europeans would give up anything in trading. They wouldn't want to go into the grave with their guns and iron tools.

Yvonne D. (age 13)

What brain research is telling educators is that the mind will learn, especially when students are actively involved in the learning process, taking responsibility for and making many of the decisions related to their own learning. Rather than being separated from their past and present experiences, students need to use those contexts as entry points into new experiences and new discoveries. They can then extend the search for meaning by exploring all the connections, especially emotional, that an experience invokes. What brain research is telling educators is that personal response is an essential ingredient in the learning process.

2 * What's happening in integrated studies?

Since the educational establishment discovered the concept of integrated or interdisciplinary studies, schools have been in a state of flux. Classroom teachers have been barraged by whatever curricular reorganizations, subject restructurings, team approaches, or classroom strategies are deemed necessary to encourage, entice, or even force them into an integrative mind-set. Unparalleled in the educational community is the degree to which anything is possible and everything is negotiable, except the status quo.

What educational theorists seem to forget, however, is that they didn't invent integrated studies. Learners did. A long time ago. Learning is an active, creative process. Most definitions of ideal learners emphasize that they are independent, self-motivated individuals who have the ability to find and solve their own problems. They are capable of inquiry, analysis, synthesis, and evaluation. In other words, they integrate their learning naturally.

As we have seen, such learners are objectively and profoundly aware of their own learning processes. Their empowerment comes through the acquisition of a complex set of sophisticated, metacognitive skills. Personal response is uniquely suited to foster those skills across the curriculum, cutting across artificial boundaries of subjects and timetables, and mirroring the natural processes of the mind itself. Through personal response, students can discover, clarify, assess, reflect on, resolve, synthesize, and refine what they really think and feel about their experiences.

The role that personal response can play in integrating the curriculum comes into sharper focus against the backdrop of the current integrated studies movement. As will become evident, rather than replace what is presently being implemented, personal response forms the perfect complement, untangling and explicating the many conflicts, inconsistencies, and incongruities with which integrated studies abound.

Why integrate?

An integrated studies approach to learning is advocated for two main reasons: the approach recognizes the way the mind actually operates, and it resolves the inherent artificialities of the traditional, curricular organization. As research results accumulate, the crucial language emerges in such familiar phrases as the following:

> *The mind searches for patterns and connections.*
> *Learning is a purposeful activity rooted in the search for meaning.*
> *Learning is inextricably tied to an individual's need to make sense of reality.*

Conversely, the traditional curriculum is attacked for being overloaded, fragmented, and too often removed from the context of the real world.

The obvious solution might seem to be to blur and remove the barriers separating traditional subject areas, making it easier to identify and pursue essential meaningful learning. Functional priorities would then determine structural form. The obvious difficulty with that solution at first was the entrenched implacability of the established curricular structures. With the relentless will to effect change in education subsequently displayed by educators and public alike, however, external structures have been redrawn, reshaped, and even removed with an ease and speed never before seen.

Less obvious but even more crucial is the problem of what to do once external barriers no longer impede integration. If nothing changes at the classroom level, at the point at which the curriculum meets the child, nothing substantial has been gained. The struggle to find an effective model of an integrated learning approach has been tortuous and fitful. The various proposed models all have inherent strengths and weaknesses.

Integrated models

Themes

When two or more solutions to the same problem are possible, Occam's razor advocates choosing the simplest solution requiring as few assumptions as possible. Organizing learning around themes is easily the simplest, most accessible, and most readily apparent of all the approaches to integrated learning. Complicating and confusing the issue of themes, however, is that not everyone agrees on what the approach actually entails. The most popular and, not coincidentally, the easiest approach to implementation simply extends what has been going on in primary programs for a long time.

Teachers of young children already use themes widely. In fact, they commonly organize cross-curricular units on the basis of themes. By selecting a particular topic and using that focus to integrate all aspects of their program, teachers attempt to better encourage, support, and reinforce children's learning. From the point of view of the child, reading, writing, listening, and speaking are all inherent aspects of the same process. Since children themselves see no differences among the language-based activities and intrinsically employ visual arts, dramatic arts, and manipulation of materials for similar purposes, the use of themes mirrors the integrated nature of their learning. In this sense, whole language and whole learning are inseparable.

Since children's inherent predilection is towards an integrated approach to learning, the use of themes allows them to use their understanding in one area of the program to unlock and further develop their understanding in another. Each additional, related experience is meant to mature, deepen, and reinforce insights previously gained. A simple example would be the study of farm animals. Activities could include visiting a pet farm, singing animal songs, reading both aloud and independently from a range of genres, writing stories, picture-making, or role-playing.

By choosing themes that reflect the interests of most young people and ensuring that the activities are open-ended and sufficiently individualized to accommodate the children's natural developmental ranges, teachers can modify and manipulate their learning/teaching environments to maximize learning opportunities. The sole purpose of a thematic approach is to organize and facilitate learning. The theme is a means to an end and must never become an end in itself.

27

Problems with themes

When transferred to the context of older learners, critical complications arise. Theoretically, themes are limited only by the imagination and inventiveness of teachers and students alike. The only prerequisite is that the themes be wide-ranging enough in appeal that all students "buy into" them to a certain extent. With older students, such themes are hard to find. As children grow older, they become more diverse in their interests, abilities, experiences, and preferred learning styles. Whether it's "the circus" or "garbage" the task of finding a universally interesting, engaging, and motivating theme for older students is discouraging, to say the least.

In the name of accountability and equity, administrators have also immersed schools in the process of establishing "outcomes". The manner in which outcomes are defined, however, can either enhance or narrow the learning experience. In the case of themes, teachers are frequently forced to identify specific, observable outcomes prior to implementing a thematic unit and then connect, sequence, or "web" the learning to maximize the incidents of integration. Objectives are written to cover the subject-specific content from areas such as mathematics, visual arts, or English. The evaluation component is then keyed to the observable and predetermined outcomes that signify reaching those objectives. As Walter Loban once observed, "The curriculum inevitably shrinks to the boundaries of evaluation; if your evaluation is narrow and mechanical, that is what your curriculum will be."

The learning derived from this kind of teacher-designed, -directed and -controlled experience must necessarily be truncated. Any classroom contains a vast complex of variables, combining the diversity of individual students and how they separately perceive and interact with their world and with each other. Students vary dramatically in self-esteem, in learning readiness, and in intellectual, emotional, and psychomotor development. To try to narrow and distill this volatile, unpredictable, and incredibly potent dynamic to a few observable outcomes and contain it within the confines of the study of "bicycles" or "The Depression" is counterproductive, if not impossible.

Another serious drawback teachers are experiencing with the theme approach is that not all subject areas are equally pertinent to any particular theme. Superficial, artificial, and inappropriate connections consequently result. The mathematical content of a study of myths, for example, would be forced and limited. Too often, pointless busy-work is assigned in one area simply to claim integration with another area. The dominant belief seems to be that any kind of integration is better than no integration at all.

In the same vein and overriding these problems is the concern many teachers hold for the development of literacy in the face of themes. When theorists claim that anything and everything is negotiable in the necessity for change, they are being irresponsible and short-sighted. The external structure must always facilitate and never militate against the learning process. In other words, the function must always dictate the form.

If one of the goals is the development of reading fluency, a theme would need to accommodate what is known about achieving that goal. In this case, overwhelming evidence indicates that reading programs should include the following components:

- materials to match individual student interests and abilities

- frequent opportunities for students to self-select materials

- a regular and significant amount of in-class time for students to simply read (as opposed to answering questions based on their reading)

- frequent opportunities for students to respond to materials in a personally significant manner

- frequent opportunities for students to discuss with someone else what they're reading

- the flexibility to employ a variety of strategies to comprehend material

Self-selection of reading materials to match individual interests and abilities promotes reading fluency; in the same vein, self-selection of content and form is also one of the basic principles of the writing process. Reading assigned novels about the Depression years or writing essays about pollution are inadequate substitutes for a contemporary and comprehensive literacy program. Add in what is known about the development of listening, speaking, and viewing and the implications for integrated or multidisciplinary studies of all kinds are clear.

Since language and learning are so intrinsically linked, some theorists are tempted to say that the learning process itself will automatically take care of literacy. Such a stance reveals ignorance of what we know about the development of language and sometimes leads to the reduction of language learning instruction to rote practice. And yet the principles of language learning are as important for adolescent learners as they are for primary or junior children.

"Meta-themes"

Other theorists suggest broadening and deepening the nature of themes to merge subject areas and reinforce the basic concept of the search for interconnected patterns. Such metacurricular themes might organize study in terms of relatively abstract concepts such as metaphor, myth, hierarchies, or problem-solving. While meta-themes might possess more intellectual integrity than the more common, topical variety, they still fall prey to the same practical problems when implemented.

Problems with meta-themes

As well as the difficulties involved in finding teachers who understand what such units might entail and determining the age groups and levels at which they might be attempted, questions also arise about the manner in which learning in this way would unfold. Integrative learning necessitates a move from a transmission or mechanistic approach in which skills, knowledge, and values are simply memorized by students to a transformational approach in which a recognition of the interrelatedness of phenomena results in personal and social change.

Meta-themes, on the other hand, appear more transactional in nature, relying on problem-solving and the scientific method. A unit on hierarchies, for example, would be framed in some sort of research model in which questions are asked, information gathered from a range of alternative sources, the information organized, the questions answered, and the whole process publicized. While this kind of process could certainly be worthwhile, it wouldn't necessarily be transformational for those involved.

Correlated studies

In this multidisciplinary approach, different teachers examine their subject areas for possible cross-curricular correlations and then plan simultaneous activities to take advantage of those correlations. In this model, the history teacher, for example, might be covering the study of aboriginal people of North America, while the English teacher read aloud from *Bury My Heart at Wounded Knee*, and the science teacher looked at the environmental impact of the arrival of Europeans. Other teachers would become involved to the extent each deemed relevant.

Problems with correlated studies

On the surface, the student is offered reinforcement and a variety of contexts for new learning. The presentation of the unit, on the other hand, remains untouched and unchanged. Whatever these teachers would have done separately, they now do at the same time. If a limited number of behavioristic outcomes are articulated prior to the learning and the evaluation system tied to those outcomes, the possibilities for students to make their own connections and see their own patterns are drastically curtailed. While certainly collaborative, the process is hardly integrative unless the teachers work closely together to reinforce the learning in all areas.

Fused studies

In a fused course of study, actual subject areas are merged. History and English could be fused, for example, and the learning in both organized around a time period or themes, such as colonization or war. In this integrated studies approach, the focus is on the real world rather than on subject areas per se. Fusion requires a sophisticated, knowledgeable, and confident staff to maintain the skills, interest, and relevance necessary to serve the needs of the learner.

Problems with fused studies

Once again the external structure developed to organize learning cannot guarantee or even direct the nature of the learning/teaching environment itself. As with themes and correlated studies, what really has to change in the classroom to accommodate a fused curriculum? The same material can be recycled in the same way, but packaged in a different container. Take the most ideal of fusions — history and geography. If the history of North America and the geography of North America are fused into one course called North

American studies, the one North American studies teacher will now probably do exactly what two teachers previously did and probably in the same way, given that a certain amount of correlation and integration may be inevitable.

Not surprisingly, the major objection to a fused model occurs when English or language arts is one component of a fused course. When self-selection of content and form is one of the basic principles of a writing process and when self-selection of reading materials to match individual interests and abilities promotes reading fluency, contemporary literacy programs will have a difficult time surviving most fused units.

Other models

The next two models grew out of attempts to motivate students to learn. Since many classroom programs had few links to students' actual lives and often prevented them from pursuing avid personal interests, educators seized on those faults as justification for creating curricula based totally on students' lives and interests.

LIFE SKILLS STUDIES

The problems and issues arising from the students' lives and world form the core of this interdisciplinary approach. Skills and knowledge from relevant staff members are utilized as students deal with such concerns as peer pressure, family life, sexuality, sexism, or the world of work.

LEARNER-DIRECTED STUDIES

In this model, the learners immerse themselves in a particular, chosen field of study and allow the problems, enthusiasms, and issues related to that field to direct the learning. In theory, a student who loves animals would move naturally into studies of the environment and its effect on animal life, animal themes in literature, or the historical importance of animals such as the buffalo or the beaver. The strength of this approach is the student-centred focus and the potential for real integration.

Problems with other models

Both models have strengths that point out some underlying problems with contemporary programs. Students learn in the context of their own specific lives and interests. When an experience is presented to a class of students, the understanding of that experience is immediately and necessarily fragmented into thirty or more different interpretations. As with witnesses to a robbery who disagree on what actually happened, personal subjectivity colors the events in a classroom. Until the personal qualities of each individual's understanding are recognized and resolved, no common understanding is possible. Devising courses that revolve wholly around students' lives and interests simply substitutes one fragmented, unbalanced approach for another.

LIFE SKILLS STUDIES

This type of approach makes a better course than it does a curriculum. The focus speaks more to adolescent mentoring than it does to a comprehensive and all-inclusive learning/teaching environment. In attempting to solve the neglect of relevance in contemporary curricula, these experiments make relevance the overriding criterion. Besides throwing out the baby with the bath-water, they leave the concepts of learning and growth locked in the temporary, subjective, and necessarily limited perspective of the adolescent. Relevance must be an integral part of integrated studies, but adolescent learners are not always the best judges of what, in the long run, may or may not be relevant.

LEARNER-DIRECTED STUDIES

Again, this approach makes a better independent study unit than it does a curriculum. As students grow older, their interests diverge. As anyone who has worked with adolescent students will attest, many of them simply do not have one overriding, all-consuming academic interest. Besides, substituting individually fused studies for one common fused study doesn't change the nature of the inquiry. The problems inherent in fused studies in general are still unresolved.

If a student does have one overriding, all-consuming passion, moreover, everything that student experiences is naturally and inherently perceived through the filter of that passion. How could it be otherwise? Any piercing interest acts like a searchlight to explain and illuminate new experiences. That kind of passion engenders personal response. Integration is unavoidable. Why reinvent the wheel?

Personal response facilitates integration

Thinking and language are inseparable. People use language to make sense of and to cope with their world. As students examine, organize, think through, and reflect on what and how they learn, they need to use their own form of language in whatever mode — transactional, expressive, poetic, or a blend — serves their purposes. ("Their own form of language" refers directly and significantly to the natural, spontaneous language students use every day.)

Rather than develop structures to explicitly include students' personal lives and interests, teachers need only offer opportunities to students to use their own language to make connections with their own lives. Students can do nothing else but respond from the context of their real-life experiences and with the passion of their individual interests. (Evaluation, of course, is an essential ingredient in this whole process. As well as intrinsic rewards, in order to be successful, the personal response package must also offer extrinsic rewards. See **Chapter 3** for implementation and **Chapter 5** for evaluation.)

Sample response to an individual interest

The form of a personal response should be dictated by the purpose. An all-consuming passion for anything and everything to do with space, from science fiction to astronomy, prompted this next expressive response. Other than a few simple shape poems, such as acrostic and concrete poems, this student claimed to have never written a poem before. He discovered that the indelible sense of wonder and unquenchable fascination with life's essential mysteries made the choice of poetry for this response inevitable.

The immediate stimuli were found in a visit to a "Trekkie" convention and a classroom discussion in a science period about surviving on the moon. The theme, format, and response itself were all by choice. Although the sentiments are vivid, sincere, and admirable, the significant point about this poem and how and why it was produced is that it happens all the time when response journals are used effectively. Independent learners pose and answer their own questions in their own ways.

Response to space

Black and dark,
Bright and light,
Large as the imagination,
The stars,
The planets,
Is there life!!
We may never know.
It is a wonderful kind of
Beauty our eyes cannot see.

Galaxies that go beyond
The human equation,
Travelling through space,
Never reaching the end.

Faces indescribably alien.
I look out at night.
I see only darkness.
Perhaps what the aliens see
Is alien to me.

What are we compared to space?
Everything?
Nothing?
Perhaps a speck on a blanket.

Space.
What a mystery!
Maybe we want to know too much.
Space will be there
When we are gone.
And it will remain
Until the end of time.

Eric J. (age 13)

Although Eric chose to craft a poetic response, most student entries in a response journal program will be necessarily informal and uncrafted. Across the curriculum, when students are learning *through* language, their use of language will often be hesitant, tentative, halting, repetitive, and recursive. The goal is understanding. As students try to make sense of themselves, their world, and their place in it, they need to observe, talk, listen, read, write, do, value, and reflect in an intricate web of related interactions.

However educators choose to organize and structure curricula, they must recognize that, within each framework, students must negotiate their learning in personally significant ways. Learning often appears messy, but only because, as outsiders, we can't trace and identify the myriad simultaneous, personally purposeful connections being made.

Sample response to a personally significant issue

The Forbidden City by William Bell is a historical novel set in China during the Tiananmen Square uprising. When this student independently read the novel, he gained a new perspective of his own life. Events from his past, personal research, and a growing understanding of the socio-political realities of the adult world merge in this remarkable response journal entry.

Response to a historical novel

I loved and hated this book all at the same time as I read it. I cannot explain it. As I read this book, I felt rage inside me. I could not believe that all that took place in Tiananmen Square on June 4. I feel like ripping the face off the person who ordered the army to fire on unarmed student demonstrators. Did you know that the students were considered outlaws and bad elements? And that if they were arrested they could be shot? As I read and read the book, I became more disgusted with the Chinese government. Outside reporters were beaten up badly if they were caught filming the massacre and then shipped off to their home country.

The aftermath of the massacre was not for nothing however. I read in the magazine, "Scholastic Scope", that the Chinese government really took the demonstration seriously. They feared a rebellion from the people so they put the situation first on their priority list. Some changes have been made in China since, but China is still a communist country and people are still fighting for democracy.

I went to a lot of the rallies in Nathan Phillips Square, downtown, when I was only ten. I did not fully understand why my parents were making me go to all those demonstrations, but now it is all clear. I just wish I had understood it while it happened.

A close estimation of how many were killed in the demonstrations in China would be about 2,000 people, not counting the soldiers killed as well. What I also read was that the Chinese government lied about the massacre. They said that more soldiers were killed than students. All lies!

Brian M. (age 13)

Personal response facilitates learning

The kinds of experiences teachers plan for their students, the outcomes they value, and the way they evaluate the process of learning should all recognize and remain congruent with the way in which students learn. In the burgeoning literature about integrated studies, two common characteristics emerge. One is a tendency to invoke the language of personal response when expressing goals, and the other is to insist on behaviorist frameworks when defining outcomes. The result is schizophrenic. By slavishly adhering to behaviorist objectives, some advocates ignore the way in which the mind learns and devalue aspects of memory and learning other than rote memorization.

People are problem-solvers. As such, they must search for patterns and relationships. People involuntarily and always integrate. If anything, in the educational community, teachers tend to underestimate and misdirect students' capacities to learn. Students carry their own themes around in their heads; they make their own connections. By ignoring the fertile diversity of students, the vast range of their interests, background experiences, abilities, and their infinite potential for making connections, behaviorist approaches obstruct rather than capitalize on the innate human need to make meaning.

It bears repeating that educational theorists did not invent integrated studies; learners did. In fact, various disciplines have always been related and tied to the real experience of life beyond the classroom. Learners always have strived and always will strive for integration. Modes of integration can either facilitate or obstruct the process, but they can't replace or stop the natural, organic process of learning. The dominant fallacy in the literature of integrated studies today is the notion that we can program that integration. From Newton in the apple orchard, making the personal connections that led to the concept of a force called gravity, to Einstein on the streetcar, seeing the patterns that connected time and space, the mind follows its own personal, idiosyncratic path to meaning. With personal response, teachers possess a comprehensive technique to track and enhance those integrative journeys.

3 * Integrating from within: Implementing response journals

Where to start

Perhaps you've tried journals before without much success or you've never used the technique and aren't sure how to begin. What do you do and how do you do it? First, the technique is, by nature, flexible. Be assured that personal response can be styled to fit your specific program, routines, and teaching style. Since no one has the one true way of implementing personal response, draw on your own knowledge and experience to adapt, discard, add to, or improve on the suggestions, cueing questions, and instruments offered here. With *your* students and in *your* learning/teaching environment, you are the acknowledged authority.

Second, personal response is all about a particular way of viewing and using language. In any program, students need opportunities to learn through using language in personally significant ways. "Learning through language" is not just a "parenthood" platitude. The process is detailed and specific and it speaks directly to learning across the curriculum. As you reflect on the following basic principles of learning through language, consider how closely they match the principles involved in using response journals.

- To fully understand concepts, students need to "pick away" at ideas or think aloud in their own talk or style of writing. Opportunities to talk and write are crucial to real learning.

- Students should feel free to take risks as they talk and write. They need to write in their own words and feel confident that the meaning of what they say is the focal point of the writing experience.

- During the talking and writing process, ideas should be examined, analyzed, reformulated, and defined in very personal, individual, and essential ways.

- The jargon of specialized subjects and needlessly technical language tend to inhibit real learning.

With response journals, students can interact with issues and materials regardless of the subject area. The forum is ideal for "examining, analyzing, reformulating, and defining" in a personal and individual manner. The technique incorporates real problems to solve, encourages students to reflect on events, ideas, and values they're confronting every day, and supports the proliferation of real purposes for talking and writing. Whatever the subject area, the skills and goals are the same. If overlap occurs, it can only reinforce the learning.

Although personal response can be stimulated in much the same way in any classroom and under any conditions, *where* that personal response is physically recorded is a variable. Teachers may be working completely independently in a single subject area or with responsibilities for two or more subject areas. They may be teaching collaboratively in teams of two or more, either permanently or, for the purposes of covering a specific unit, temporarily. They may be working on a theme or in a correlated- or fused-studies situation. Whatever the context, a routine for recording personal response needs to be developed.

As mentioned earlier, the journal could be a separate notebook or a section in a notebook. A group of teachers could share a notebook or a personal response section of a binder, or a subject-specific notebook could have a separate, personal response section. Whatever the arrangement, the only restriction is that students must be aware of the personal response process and must have some kind of recording routine to accommodate both the process and the evaluation of that process.

How to cue personal response

Independent learners have little difficulty deciding for themselves how best to respond to materials and ideas in a personally significant manner; they merely need the opportunity. Most students, however, are unused to accepting responsibility for processing the experience they've had from a lesson, a film, an experiment, or a discussion. They look to the teacher to tell them "what to do now". They see the process of learning as matching a prescribed set of answers someone else knows to a prescribed set of questions someone else devises.

Such students may, at first, appreciate a few model or sample questions to cue their initial efforts. Gradually, they will accept more and more responsibility for their responses. Some students will require more support and a longer "settling in" period than others. As students become more independent and begin to accept their own autonomy in the learning process, they should be weaned from an unbudging reliance on a list of questions. If they aren't, the responses tend to become formulary and even perfunctory.

Essential here is the understanding that direction from the teacher is not only acceptable in personal response, but necessary. Some teachers have expressed concern about interfering in the learning process or narrowing the scope by assigning a specific response to the class as a whole or by criticizing either the form or content of a response. On the contrary, intervention is part of the process.

Teachers need to guide students through to an awareness that meaningful reflection is the goal, not simply writing responses. They need to illustrate for students how specific responses can be strengthened to achieve that end (See **Chapter 5, Evaluating personal response**, pages 73-89). They need to discuss with their students how frequently and thoughtfully students are responding, as well as dealing with the form those responses are taking. On occasion, teachers even need to assign specific responses.

The following sample cueing questions are intended to stimulate response to three categories of classroom activity: a generic lesson; a hands-on experience, such as an experiment, an activity in design and technology, or a mathematical construction; and a film or video. The cueing questions for responding to discussions are found in the chapter dealing comprehensively with the entire issue of small-group, co-operative learning (See **Chapter 4, Integrating co-operative learning**, pages 58-72).

Too many choices are often as bad as too few. The long lists of cueing questions would be intimidating or confusing for someone just starting with personal response. **Directions to students** and an abbreviated list of cueing questions are provided for each category of responses to introduce the concept in a more focused manner. As the copyright notice at the bottom of each **Directions to Students** indicates, the entire page may be reproduced for classroom use. Completing the categories are sample student responses.

Remember that the following sample questions are suggestions only and are intended only for students who choose to use them.

Responding to a Lesson

Sample Cueing Questions

• What have you already thought about or experienced as far as this issue or topic is concerned? How has today's lesson clarified, confused, or changed what you already thought or knew?

• What especially surprised, interested, or impressed you today? What more do you hope to learn about this issue or topic?

• What questions do you still have about this issue or topic?

• Tell about a television program, either documentary or fictional, that dealt with this issue or topic and what you learned from it.

• In your own neighborhood and among your own friends and family, what importance or relevance does this issue or topic have? How could it be made more relevant to your situation?

• What have you read in newspapers or magazines, heard on the news, or talked to people about as far as this issue or topic is concerned?

• What would you have liked more of in today's lesson and why would you want that? What would you have liked less of and why?

• Where do you personally stand on this issue or topic? What are your views, opinions, and beliefs and why do you think the way you do?

• Pretend you are a character experiencing what was discussed today. Write in role as that person. What are you doing, thinking, and feeling?

• What feelings did you experience in response to today's lesson (e.g., irritation, disbelief, recognition, wonder) and why do you think you responded that way?

• What kind of response do you feel like making to today's lesson or issue (e.g., a poem, a word web, a drawing or diagram, a letter to the editor)?

Directions to Students

Responding to a Lesson

As we sit through a lesson, our minds can be activated in a variety of ways. Sometimes, questions come up that might not be answered, a difference of opinion arises that isn't cleared up, or we want to say something and just don't get the chance. Our minds often linger on those questions, opinions, or ideas long after the course of the lesson has changed. Sometimes, our minds jump from idea to idea or memory to memory and we aren't really sure what the connection is.

Now that the lesson is completed, try to describe what was happening in your mind. The place to start is your own personal reaction and how and why your mind reacted the way it did. Some people have found the following kinds of questions useful in guiding their responses. These are only suggestions. Your own response may not be covered by these questions.

During the lesson:

• What questions or comments came to mind? Don't worry about how "important" the detail or issue may be; if it's on your mind, it's important enough.

• What was there about the lesson that involved you the most? What especially surprised, interested, or impressed you today? What more do you hope to learn about this issue or topic?

• What feelings did you experience in response to today's lesson (e.g., irritation, disbelief, recognition, wonder) and why do you think you responded that way?

Sample response to a lesson

The emotional element of racism shapes how we deal with the issue. Although we try to deal intellectually and objectively with racism in any number of subject areas and topics, we also need to free the emotions of our students to foster awareness, reflection, analysis, and real understanding.

When the following response moves from an external, intellectual perspective to a personal, experiential perspective, the emotional subtext reveals how perplexing the issue can be. It's important to realize that the student is herself Chinese.

Response to a history lesson

Racism is going around badly in this country. Everyone hates each other for their skin color. There are lots of fights between different people. Racism is unfair to people. It affects the next generation badly because it teaches the kids or offspring to dislike each other when they grow up. I feel parents are a great influence to their kids. If parents start hating someone from a different nation, their kids will learn from them. Racism also hurts people, and not just physically. It makes people mad at not only a person, but also the whole group. Nowadays, there are many examples of racism in our lives.

I was strolling in the Chinese mall with my few friends. An English person came through the doorway. She was a pretty girl, two big, blue eyes, long, loose, yellow hair, and white, smooth skin. Many people stared at her, not because she was so pretty, but because she was a different skin color. She looked quite isolated. No one talked to her. No one smiled at her. I felt really sorry for her. I hated Chinese, even myself. Why can't we be friendly with each other? Why are we always attacking each other? Why can't we be peaceful with each other? I feel very confused.

Li Li W. (age 13)

Responding to a Hands-On Experience

Sample Cueing Questions

• What did you do today, what did you learn, and how did you feel about it?

• If you were to give advice or directions to someone new to this activity, what helpful hints would you offer?

• What did you find most difficult about what you did today and why was it so difficult? What was easiest for you and why?

• What sensations were you aware of (e.g., sounds, colors, textures, temperature, materials)? When have you noticed similar sensations and under what circumstances?

• If you could make a video of today's experience, what close-ups would you like to see, what parts would you spend the most time shooting, and what would you edit out?

• What experiences have you had before that reminded you of what you did today and why did you make those connections?

• What did you most enjoy today and why did you enjoy it so much? What did you enjoy least and why?

• When would you use this kind of experience in your own life, how would you use it, and of what use would it be?

• If you could take one photograph of today's activity, what would it be? Draw a picture of the photograph.

Directions to Students

Responding to a Hands-On Experience

Some of the most vivid impressions we ever have occur when we are actively involved in doing something. Images of textures, colors, and sounds run through our minds, often mixed up with odd thoughts and related memories. Sometimes, whatever we're thinking is clearly stimulated by what we're doing. At other times, the link isn't immediately apparent.

After the activity today, what kinds of questions, impressions, feelings, or comments are left in your mind? How would you describe the experience, what you've learned, and the value it's had for you? The place to start is your own personal reaction and how and why your mind reacted the way it did.

Some people have found the following kinds of questions useful in guiding their responses. These are only suggestions. Your own response may not be covered by these questions.

• What sensations were you aware of today (e.g., sounds, colors, textures, temperature, materials)? When have you noticed similar sensations and under what circumstances?

• If you were to give advice or directions to someone new to this activity, what helpful hints would you offer?

• If you could take one photograph of today's activity, what would it be? Draw a picture of that photograph.

• What did you do today, what did you learn, and how did you feel about it?

Sample responses to a hands-on experience

Some of the most startling, perceptive, and revealing responses stem from hands-on experiences. Whether a science experiment, a mathematical construction, or an art activity, the concrete manipulation of objects and the engagement of all the senses can unleash a host of memories, associations, and feelings. The merging of an individual's intellectual, emotional, and physical perceptions tends to make these experiences immediate, powerful, and resonant.

This response followed a lesson on metal-working. Even a year after the initial experience, the impressions remain specific and vivid. The memories of the design and technology shop will certainly linger long after the metal-working lesson that stimulated them.

Response to design and technology activity

I have worked with steel in metal shops; that was last year but I still remember it. I remember welding two pieces of metal together with the help of a torch. I was afraid to light the torch at first, but then I got used to it. To get a good flame that's very hot you make the orange flame long with smoke coming out. Them you add oxygen to make it very blue. I know that I will always remember to turn off the torch because one time I forgot and I burned my finger pretty badly.

The metal shop was interesting because every time I learned a bit more, like using certain types of tools to cut or bend certain types and sizes of metal. I have an uncle who works as a mechanical engineer. I'm not quite sure if he works with steel or not.

Wendy H. (age 14)

The importance of hands-on experience in learning is as often underestimated as is the affective or emotional content intrinsic to all learning. Both ingredients are charmingly and spontaneously revealed in the next response. The student expresses an unfortunate emotional reaction to a previous learning episode; she developed a dislike for prisms. After a series of hands-on experiences in constructing geometric forms and decorating them with personal data and graphics, however, she had a change of heart.

The concrete manipulations and the opportunity to individualize the experience gave her a solid basis for visualizing, remembering, and reflecting on this particular shape. Her response clearly articulates a new, emotional involvement. An interest in the correct spelling of the shape and a heightened interest in other geometric forms accompanies her revised, positive feelings. The interaction with the teacher near the end of the response is a characteristic of responses from students who seek out a more personal relationship with the teacher through frequent dialogues in their journal.

Response to mathematics (geometry)

A prism is one object that I didn't really like, but now I really like it. It has a lot of faces and the lines are parallel. The faces are all flat. I enjoy doing things with prisms now because when they ask you in a test or a book what a prism is like you can tell them right away. Prism is kind of a hard word to spell for people because when you sound it out, it sounds like this — "prisim" — when it actually is spelled like this — prism. A prism is not that popular an object. What is your favourite object? My favourite is a prism. Lots of people like the square. Do you like the square? I know why lots of people like the square. Do you?

Annesa R. (age 11)

Sample response to a hands-on lesson

A contradiction exists in the way most teachers talk about gym or physical education and what they actually do about it. While they invoke the belief that physical activity can build self-esteem and foster essential collaborative skills and values, they tend to isolate whatever happens in the gym or on the playing field from the rest of the curriculum.

Two examples follow to illustrate how personal response can focus and deepen a learning experience in physical education, as well as promote the reflective practice that broadens the learning. Through response journals, these experiences are easily transferred to the larger curriculum.

Response to volleyball

In this first, brief example, the student communicates the exhilarating joy of a sudden flash of achievement, connects that achievement to practice, and resolves to embrace the new skill as often as possible. This insight into self-esteem, confidence, process, and achievement needs to be shared and generalized.

In gym, I learned how to spike a volleyball. Ms. K. kept making me practice and finally I got it! I always wanted to know how to spike one and now I can.

I remember it so clearly. I jammed the ball so hard straight down on to the ground. Now every time I play volleyball I want to spike it.

Nat R. (age 12)

Like many other students, the next individual is a product of competitive sports and inter-school competition. Unlike the previous student, he is a gifted athlete. In his world, the more proficient you are individually, the more your team will win, and the more status and acclaim you will garner. Teamed with the best players in the school, he is used to winning.

Introduced to a daily random picking of teams during physical education classes and an emphasis on the enjoyment of playing, rather than on simply winning, Scott entered a period of personal conflict. His response journal entry recounts his struggles to sort out his competitive instincts and his evolving understanding of the nature of collaboration.

Response to floor hockey

I've learned how to take losing a little better even if we lose 10-1 or so because I would think that I could still get a goal or an assist if I tried hard. I'm still short-fused, but I control my temper a little better.

I was surprised when I stopped mouthing off when I lost and stopped losing my temper. I was impressed by our team work and the results we got even though the talent just wasn't there. I had to play a lot of different positions. I never realized before that I have the hard shot and the stick-handling of a rushing defence player. I felt good about my teammates because I still emerged as a bit of a star player and so I knew I'd get the playing time I wanted and people in my class recognized that I could be dangerous in the offensive zone.

I also started to realize that team play and being a good sport is the key to enjoying sports. And sometimes individual performance makes me feel better than winning the game.

Scott S. (age 12)

Responding to a Film or Video

Sample Cueing Questions

• If you were the writer/director of this film, how would you change the content or the presentation?

• If you were going to show this film to someone else, what would you tell them to look for?

• When you think about this film, what comes to mind? What comes next? What web of associations can you develop?

• How did this film add to or clarify what you already knew, thought, or felt about this topic?

• After viewing this film, what questions spring to mind that you would like answered about either the topic or issues or the way they were covered?

• What facts, issues, or sections seemed confusing or difficult to understand right away? What would you like clarified?

• When you consider the ideas presented, the arguments, and the point of view, what do you strongly agree or disagree with in this film and why do you feel the way you do?

• What connections did you make between your own life and experiences and what was presented in the film?

• What is important to you about the film and what would you like to say about it?

• Would you like to see this film again? Why or why not?

Directions to Students

Responding to a Film or Video

As you think about this film, don't worry about whether or not you've remembered everything you think you should have or what somebody else might think is important. Don't worry about retelling everything in it or even talking about whether or not the film was "good" or "bad". Instead, concentrate on the images, facts, and situations that first come to mind and what they made you start thinking about.

It what you want to say about the film isn't clear, try reflecting on some of these question. Remember that they are only suggestions.

• After viewing this film, what questions spring to mind that you would like answered about either the topic or issues or the way they were covered?

• If you were the writer/director of this film, how would you change the content or the presentation?

• If you were going to show this film to someone else, what would you tell them to look for?

• When you think about this film, what first comes to mind? What comes next? What web of associations can you develop?

Sample response to a film or video

Since all films are shaped by and, to varying degrees, present a point of view purposely fashioned by the makers of the film, even the relatively objective nature of documentaries, nature films, and other educational films have a subjective impact. Besides, a film or video is a complex mixture of sound, motion, and picture. The barrages of images, words, and ideas serve more as triggers for our own memories and associations than as unfettered conduits for pure ideas. Comprehension occurs in the mind as an individual begins to analyze the vicarious experience through the filter of real-life experiences and the beliefs and values formed from them.

Students need to be reassured that these subjective, personal impressions are valid and important entry points into an examination of a film's content and presentation. In the following response to a film shown in a geography class, the student displays a healthy scepticism reinforced by the graphic nature of the images. The film dealt with the origins of aboriginal North Americans and their migration from Siberia to North America over the Bering Strait. A number of images of glaciers and the frozen arctic wastes were included.

Response to a geography film

I know those scientists know their business, but I don't see how they know so much about what happened 20,000 years ago from bones. They weren't even human bones. They were just animal bones. It seemed a little bizarre that they were sitting around cracking open the bones of an elephant to prove that what they said about the old animal bones was true. I thought scientists had machines and things and here they were sitting in a circle breaking elephant bones! What about that stuff about native people walking over to Alaska from Siberia? The ice was piled up like mountains! They didn't have any trees or animals or shelter or anything else. I've been up to my cottage in the winter and I wouldn't want to live outside there and this was worse. How could they live? Why would they even want to walk to a place like that?

Donna M. (age 12)

Responding to private issues

When journals first became popular in English classes, they provided a forum both for individual, exploratory writing and for privileged, non-threatening dialogue, primarily with the teacher. In their journals, students could monitor and express their own inner dialogues as they reacted either to issues and events from the classroom curriculum and the wider world or to the significant experiences and emotions arising from their private lives. This free-flowing dialogue could also be extended to teacher and peers as students felt a need to include others in their thoughts and deliberations. Sometimes they wrote to others for advice; sometimes they needed only a sympathetic and trusted reader.

When students wrote to their teachers, the teachers often responded right in the students' journals. Other teachers thoughtfully used separate pieces of paper or "stick-on" message paper to let students decide whether or not to retain the replies in the journals. In any event, the journals acted as a safety valve for students, allowing them to tap powerful feelings and, when they were in the grip of serious and often confusing personal problems, to express those feelings to someone else. Although the implementation and maintenance of these early journals was often misguided, those functions of the journals were vitally needed.

Now the use of response journals has spread even more. In the face of integrated curricula and structures, moreover, teachers across the curriculum are expected to fill the role of trusted adult. Almost anyone using journals should expect that some students at some time will reach out, through their journal entries, to a sympathetic, trusted, and responsive adult. While they would prefer that journals be viewed, for the most part, as another type of notebook, most teachers would also like to encourage and support the vital private function of journals.

The move to an integrated curriculum has, at least, placed the focus in education squarely on the learner; courses and units of

54

study, in and of themselves, have value only in relation to the nature and needs of the learner. The more teachers are aware of the personal lives and private worlds of their students, the more effectively they can adjust the learning/teaching environment to take that background into account. More to the point, teachers have a responsibility to attend to the physical, emotional, and intellectual well-being of their students.

Guidelines for private response

In order to encourage this kind of personal writing and an exchange of perspectives, either student to student or student to teacher, a few basic guidelines need to be observed.

- Response journals belong to the students. This basic principle ensures the confidentiality of the private aspects of the response journals. Non-confidential content such as to what extent a student is achieving the personal response objectives can certainly be shared with others at the teacher's discretion. Although the response journals are read and marked by the teacher, they should always be returned to the student. Of course, if students choose to share the contents with others, they certainly may.

- Essentially private writing must never be marked either for content or for form. Such entries should be clearly marked *private*.

- Students must be reassured that in spite of existing routines for reading response journals, teachers will always welcome and read a private entry at any time, if the student feels it's pressing and important enough to hand in. Again, such entries should be clearly marked *private*.

- With writing of a private nature, teachers must always respond in the role of trusted adult. In this role, teachers may often walk a tightrope with their comments. They need to advise but not command, disagree but not reject, and sympathize but not condone. In effect, they need to respond as adult friend to student friend.

When acquainting students with this added feature of response journals, teachers may want to use the following formal introduction. Once discussed, the page can be included in the journal pages or discarded.

Directions to Students

Responding to Private Issues

Everyone needs a friend to talk to. But you don't have to have a friend in order to sort out what's on your mind. You can "talk about" your thoughts and feelings with yourself and with your teacher/reader — in your response journals. Remember to mark *private* in your response journal whenever you want to write in this fashion. Your private entries will never be shown to anyone else without your knowledge.

If you want your teacher (or a special friend in class) to read and reply to what you've written, simply hand it in (or hand it to your friend) and ask for a response. Unless you indicate otherwise, your teacher will reply on a separate, loose-leaf page or a pad of "stick-on" message paper to allow you the option of keeping or not keeping the reply in your response journal.

When you decide to write this way, find a quiet spot and don't concern yourself with mechanics or neatness or even how well or how poorly you're wording your thoughts. Even a poorly worded entry will get you in touch with your own thoughts and feelings and show you how you felt at a certain time — and that's the point to this kind of writing. Focus on the issue or feeling or idea and write whatever comes to your mind. If you need a focus to begin, here are some suggestions.

• Explain your inner feelings. Try to put those feelings, good or bad, into words. This process can help you understand how your emotions work.

• Work out your problems. If you write about your worries, you may be able to understand more clearly what causes them.

• Explore ideas about life. Describe things you've noticed about human nature. Discuss your ideas of right and wrong. Tell what you think is important in life.

If you have something you want to write about but don't know how to start, try one of these phrases to get you going: *Right now I feel... Sometimes, I wonder if... Some day, I'm going to... I hate it when ....*

Sample response to a private issue

What follows is an excerpt from a three-page entry that started out as a response to a novel. A mention of the mark the student had received from a previous unit on storytelling led to a discussion of how important marks were to her parents. The rest of the excerpt needs no further explanation. After receiving the entry, the teacher had a private chat with the student. Guidance personnel were subsequently included in the process and the members of the family were able to confront and, eventually, resolve the conflict. Prior to the entry, neither the school staff nor the family recognized the depth of the student's unhappiness.

> If I don't get better this term, my parents will be upset and disappointed and I'll be grounded for the rest of the year. They make me feel trapped, no, closed in and I always feel they're watching me everywhere I go. Can you believe that I've had my bags packed in my closet six times! I don't want to run away forever, but long enough for them to realize what they're doing to me. They won't even let me go out the way other kids do or go to the mall. Sometimes I go a little wild, but I'm not really a head case or I don't think so anyway. That fight I had last week really sent them crazy, as if it was my fault! I don't think they'd be sorry if I left. They wouldn't even notice I was gone... If I went to the guidance counsellor with personal problems, wouldn't they think I was some kind of mental case? I wouldn't be able to talk to her like that openly because it would make me feel uncomfortable and I would forget something or get mixed up and it would be rather pointless. Maybe that's why last year I would never really, inside, get over anything. Anyway, I don't feel like I'm crazy even if I act like I'm crazy sometimes.
>
> Wanda M. (age 14)

4 * Integrating co-operative learning

In these collaborative times, the ability to operate responsibly and effectively in small-group discussion situations is a highly valued skill. Uniquely both process and product, co-operative learning is not only one of the most powerful learning/teaching strategies that educators have discovered but is also a clearly identified and universally prized outcome expected from the educational system. As such, co-operative learning is the most potent, flexible, and integrative force in schools today.

A multi-facetted process, co-operative learning can boost students' self-esteem, improve their achievement, help them attain task-oriented goals more efficiently, and even enable them to become aware of and reassess their personal value systems. For teachers, the process intrinsically cuts across disciplines and demonstrates how the responsibility for a shared set of skills and a shared outcome can be collaboratively transferred from class to class, practiced, and evaluated.

Regardless of the age or abilities of the students, the subject-specific area they're working in, or the nature or content of their discussions, the set of skills remains the same. Whether the structure of the unit is interdisciplinary, multidisciplinary, or isolated within one subject area, the practice of those skills remains essential. From all perspectives, co-operative learning strategies integrate in and of themselves, flowing in, around, and out of the learning process wherever it occurs. The medium very definitely is the message.

Sample response to collaboration

Collaboration enables the group by empowering the individual. As well as being a fine artist and an accomplished musician, the following student is gifted in all academic areas. Customarily a perfectionist and independently motivated to the point of exclusion, she relates what collaboration means to her.

> I've learned a lot this year that I've never known of. For one thing, I've enjoyed my writing. For another, I've learned to give myself breaks when things became too nerve-wracking. I've relaxed a lot and become much looser and more open with people. It's a good thing, too. I mean, had things been different I might have had a nervous breakdown at the age of 13.
>
> Mainly, I think I learned these valuable little bits when I have talked with people, like K., and R., and Mr. P., and so forth. I really like being with people and learning things from them and they learn things about themselves from me, too. Working with people makes it a beautiful and memorable time.
>
> Jenny A. (age 13)

Discussing and responding

Successful small-group discussions don't just happen; they develop as a result of careful planning, positive coaching, and lots of practice. By collaborating on a regular basis in pairs and groups of three, four, or more, students can develop the interactive skills necessary to share and build on the foundation of each other's interests, backgrounds, experiences, and insights.

Response journals have a vital role to play in this process. They can be used to focus on the dynamics of a group, regardless of the content of the discussion or task. In certain circumstances, they can also allow an individual to reflect and comment on the content of the group's investigations, extending or elaborating on a personal perspective.

Caution is advised, however, when using a written component in a small-group discussion. If there is a written component based on the content of a discussion, teachers should be sure they've articulated for themselves and for their students the purpose and the value of that component. Before examining the role of response journals in developing small-group discussion skills, consider some of the **don'ts** and **do's** of recording the content of discussions.

Some don'ts and do's

DON'T'S

- **Don't** ask students to transcribe the course of the discussion. That kind of activity is usually assigned as a test of how well students were following and contributing to the discussion. As well as undercutting and devaluing the process of the discussion, this practice forces students into needless duplication. Eventually, the attitude in the group becomes "the less we say, the less we have to write."

- **Don't** treat discussions as rehearsals for essay-writing. A discussion is a complete learning/teaching experience in itself. If you plan to have students write an essay after a discussion, the purpose for that discussion becomes preparation for writing. Obviously, there's nothing wrong with brainstorming, webbing, and other pre-writing activities. Just don't confuse them with personal response.

- **Don't** ask students to "report" on other students in their journal in terms of either what they say or how they behave. Co-operative learning operates on a basis of trust and respect. If a group is operating inefficiently, other techniques can be used to turn the experience into a positive learning opportunity.

DO'S

- **Do** ask students to record the date and topic of each discussion and the names of the members of their groups each time. This basic tracking function keeps the journal record complete and can be performed before or after a discussion. The student and teacher or team of teachers can examine the record and determine when and how often discussions have taken place, under what circumstances and with whom, and precisely what was discussed.

• **Do** give students an opportunity to record information after a discussion that they may find useful at a later date. They may want to record such items as a section in a text they need to review, surprising or intriguing comments they want to remember, a reminder to look up a disputed fact, or a sudden thought or memory stimulated by the discussion. The teacher, as well, may want to focus the reponse with cueing questions designed to stimulate a personal reaction to the content of the discussion.

• **Do** use the response journal to help students develop effective small-group discussion skills. Regularly ask them to reflect on and analyze their own behavior in group discussions, the strengths they usually display, the roles they need to develop further, and their reactions to the dynamics of being a responsible and complete group member.

• **Do** encourage students to trade, read, and, with the permission of the owner, extend a small-group discussion into a paired dialogue by corresponding in their journals. Remember, however, that the journal is a recognized and defined component of the unit of study and as such is open to the scrutiny of the supervising teacher or teachers and part of the portfolio of work that will be summatively evaluated.

Sample response to a discussion

This next response illustrates a few of the reasons why students need opportunities to extend the theme of the discussion into the response journal. The student is clearly aware of her limitations in small-group situations, an insight the teacher needs to share. In spite of those limitations, her journal allows her to give voice to a powerful and disturbing personal connection between the discussion and her own life. Certainly, the teacher will want to speak privately with her to help her explore the issues and answer the questions she's raised. Once the incident she describes has been acknowledged by her teacher, the student may risk offering the example in a later discussion.

Such a shy one. Most of the time I sit and smile. It's so difficult to be bold. Does anyone even know that I have ideas and language in my head? I can write anything in clear images but I must look so stupid to people who talk about themselves so easily and say anything on their minds. In the racism discussion today I wanted to tell about some things a man said to my father in a restaurant last week but I didn't say anything because I didn't know what they would think. You see, my father's friend owns this restaurant but he wasn't there and no one said anything to the man. Everybody just tried to ignore him and pretend he wasn't there. He was so rude and racist and no one did anything to him. Can you get someone arrested if they call you racist names in a restaurant? My father couldn't believe it. The man left and there wasn't a fight or anything but my father's going to talk to his friend and find out why no one at the restaurant said anything to him.

Jasdene S. (age 14)

Setting up groups

Group membership can be decided by the teacher, randomly, or by the participants themselves. When teachers choose who works with whom, they usually do so to redress some kind of perceived imbalance, such as the ratio of females to males, for example, or exclusionary situations such as long-standing friendships interfering with group process or groups of ESL students needing the stimulation of first-language users. Whatever the cause, these groups must never remain static. Teachers should regularly vary the groups with random and student self-selection.

A simple but effective method of creating random groups is to use colored, numbered, or lettered cards. The teacher decides, first, how many students will constitute a group and how many groups will be necessary given the size of the class. If six groups of five are needed, the teacher makes up five cards with red dots, five cards with yellow dots, and so on until all the proposed groups are accounted for. The shuffled cards are distributed. The teacher then designates areas within the classroom for each colored group to meet. The cards are collected and reused when desired.

Depending on the constitution of the class, the students' experience with small-group learning, and the comfort level of the teacher, students can be encouraged to devise their own small groups. Having at least one or two friends in a group can inject an immediate sense of security and trust for some students and encourage risk-taking. By the same token, long-standing friendships carry with them a network of accustomed behaviors, some of which may impede the work of the group.

As with all the groups, however devised, the individual members must understand the roles they need to fulfill within a group, reflect on how they perform at any one time and over a period of time, and set attainable, specific goals to improve their performance. Such reflection occurs in the response journal.

Developing small-group discussion skills

To be effective and responsible members of a small-group discussion, students need to be aware of the different roles they have to play in a group and to be given opportunities to practice them. The key small-group discussion roles are:

• sharing with others
• replying to others
• leading others
• supporting others
• evaluating in a group

Prior to a discussion, a teacher can highlight one of these roles by giving the students a few questions which establish the criteria for the skills involved. The following questions deal with how well students share with others.

- Do you share with other people your opinions, feelings, or special knowledge?

- Do you listen carefully to others so that what you know can be linked to what they know?

- When you give an opinion, do you offer the facts and reasons that support that opinion?

After the discussion, students can record in their response journals such reflections as whether or not they practiced these above skills, how well they succeeded or why they didn't, and what they would try to do in future to improve their performance in a particular response role. Remember that a student should comment only on his/her performance and **not** on a peer's.

Teachers can compare each student's observations with their own perceptions and discuss them with the student in a formative way during individual conferences. Over time, the response journal entries will present the teacher with a profile of each student's involvement in group discussions, the degree to which a student is developing self-awareness, the personal goals a student sets, and the kind of success a student is finding in particular areas.

Students should be briefed beforehand about the process. At designated intervals, the teacher can review this process and assign a summative mark based on stated criteria. (See sample summative evaluation marking sheet based on stated criteria, page 81.)

Sample response to a small-group discussion

After a small-group discussion about violence, prompted by a study of violence in the media, this student chose to elaborate on her developing insights, her strong emotional reaction, and the functioning of her particular discussion group. While it effectively sums up the discussion, her response also reflects the spontaneous, back-and-forth flow of the discussion as the group members struggled for understanding.

Response to a discussion about violence

> *I have realized that most of the teaching about violence happens very young. Children are taught to play with guns and to play war. They watch cartoons with a lot of violence, but in them, when somebody gets hit on the head, they get right back up. I can't believe that people would actually want to go to war to fight, but I suppose that's a result of the way they were brought up. I don't feel that killing people or yourself is either funny or fun. It's gross and stupid. I really hope that people realize that sitting down and talking out your problems is much better than fighting, even if the fighters are Ninja Turtles.*
>
> *Sometimes, some people can put you down and make you feel insecure. I feel that our group did well and made all of us feel better that we were able to talk out our fears and why we thought this was happening.*
>
> Nicole E. (age 12)

Highlighting particular skills

In *Learning to Work in Groups*, Matthew Miles identifies five functions that groups perform and that each group member, at various times, needs to contribute. When group members accept the responsibility for fulfilling these functions as needed, the group operates efficiently.

These discussion-group responsibilities can be isolated and highlighted for students. Some sample categories, focussing questions, and diagnostic questionnaires follow. For any single discussion, you should focus on only one of these categories. By returning to the same questions and questionnaires at intervals, you can invite students to reflect on their own progress as well as open a window on the process to assist you in your evaluation.

The small-group discussion questionnaire is a useful way to both introduce the specific targeted skills and also establish for each student an individual performance baseline. As the year progresses, the students can reassess their development in each skill, compare their functioning level with that initial baseline, and set new goals.

Additionally, prior to a discussion, one or more response roles can be highlighted. After the discussion, students record in their response journals such items as whether or not they practiced that particular skill, how well they succeeded or why they didn't, and what they would like to try to do in future discussions to improve their performance in that particular area.

Each of the five questionnaires that follow highlights a different small-group discussion skill. To gain a more complete picture of how the students customarily operate within a group, they are asked *how often* they practice each skill, *how difficult* they find it, and *how successful* they are at applying it.

Sample response to a discussion questionnaire

Developing, refining, and maintaining efficient and effective group skills is a complex process that evolves over a lifetime. Each step in that process, however small it may appear, is important. Even the resistance displayed in the following response to one of the questionnaires reveals vital information. The issues of self-esteem and fairness will need to be addressed and resolved before the student is able to become totally objective about and accept responsibility for his own performance.

I can see that I don't lead a group very often. Most of the time I don't want to because it would look like I was trying to boss people around. I can do it when I've got something important that I want to say. It's not like I'm shy or anything. You keep saying we have to do all these thing in groups. How can we do all that if we just don't have ideas and we don't have anything to say? If you didn't have listeners, talkers wouldn't have anybody to talk to. I can give my opinion the same as anybody else so I don't understand why you mark me down all the time for groups. Maybe you think I'm fooling around but I'm not fooling around any more than anybody else and they get good marks. No offence but I don't think it's a fair way to do things.

Phillip B. (age 13)

Student diagnostic discussion questionnaires

Highlighted skill: sharing with others

Name _____ Class _____

Please consider your usual performance in a small-group discussion.

Highlighted Skill: **Sharing with Others** (Please circle your choice.)

A. How often do you...(**Always, Often, Sometimes, Not Often, Never**)

1. share with other people your opinions, feelings, or
   special knowledge?   **A   O   S   N/O   N**

2. listen carefully to others so that what you know
   can be linked to what they know?   **A   O   S   N/O   N**

3. offer facts and reasons to support your opinions? **A   O   S   N/O   N**

B. How difficult is it for you to...(**Extremely, Very, Somewhat, Difficult at Times, Not Difficult at All**)

1. share with other people your opinions, feelings, or
   special knowledge?   **E   V   S   D/T   N**

2. listen carefully to others so that what you know
   can be linked to what they know?   **E   V   S   D/T   N**

3. offer facts and reasons to support your opinions? **E   V   S   D/T   N**

C. How successfully do you...(**Extremely, Very, Somewhat, Successfully at Times, Not Successfully**)

1. share with other people your opinions, feelings, or
   special knowledge?   **E   V   S   S/T   N**

2. listen carefully to others so that what you know
   can be linked to what they know?   **E   V   S   S/T   N**

3. offer facts and reasons to support your opinions? **E   V   S   S/T   N**

Highlighted skill: replying to others

Name _____ Class _____

Please consider your usual performance in a small-group discussion.

Highlighted skill: **Replying to Others** (Please circle your choice.)

A. How often do you...**(Always, Often, Sometimes, Not Often, Never)**

1. listen carefully so that you can ask clarifying
   questions or offer clarifying statements when
   necessary?   **A   O   S   N/O   N**

2. reply freely to other people's questions, interests,
   problems, and concerns?   **A   O   S   N/O   N**

3. share equally in the talking the group does?   **A   O   S   N/O   N**

B. How difficult is it for you to...**(Extremely, Very, Somewhat, Difficult at Times, Not Difficult at All)**

1. listen carefully so that you can ask clarifying
   questions or offer clarifying statements when
   necessary?   **E   V   S   D/T   N**

2. reply freely to other people's questions, interests,
   problems, and concerns?   **E   V   S   D/T   N**

3. share equally in the talking the group does?   **E   V   S   D/T   N**

C. How successfully do you... **(Extremely, Very, Somewhat, Successfully at Times, Not Successfully)**

1. listen carefully so that you can ask clarifying
   questions or offer clarifying statements when
   necessary?   **E   V   S   S/T   N**

2. reply freely to other people's questions, interests,
   problems, and concerns?   **E   V   S   S/T   N**

3. share equally in the talking the group does?   **E   V   S   S/T   N**

Highlighted skill: leading others

Name _____ Class _____

Please consider your usual performance in a small-group discussion.

Highlighted Skill: **Leading Others** (Please circle your choice.)

A. How often do you...**(Always, Often, Sometimes, Not Often, Never)**

1. suggest your own ideas, other ways to solve
   problems, or new directions for the group to
   explore?   A   O   S   N/O   N

2. make sure when you speak up that you don't cut
   someone off or interfere with the progress the
   group is making?   A   O   S   N/O   N

3. make sure when you offer suggstions that you
   don't dominate the group?   A   O   S   N/O   N

B. How difficult is it for you to...**(Extremely, Very, Somewhat, Difficult at Times, Not Difficult at All)**

1. suggest your own ideas, other ways to solve
   problems, or new directions for the group to
   explore?   E   V   S   D/T   N

2. make sure when you speak up that you don't cut
   someone off or interfere with the progress the
   group is making?   E   V   S   D/T   N

3. make sure when you offer suggstions that you
   don't dominate the group?   E   V   S   D/T   N

C. How successfully do you...**(Extremely, Very, Somewhat, Successfully at Times, Not Successfully)**

1. suggest your own ideas, other ways to solve
   problems, or new directions for the group to
   explore?   E   V   S   S/T   N

2. make sure when you speak up that you don't cut
   someone off or interfere with the progress the
   group is making?   E   V   S   S/T   N

3. make sure when you offer suggstions that you
   don't dominate the group?   E   V   S   S/T   N

Highlighted skill: supporting others

Name _____ Class _____

Please consider your usual performance in a small-group discussion.

Highlighted Skill: **Supporting Others** (Please circle your choice.)

A. How often do you...(**Always, Often, Sometimes, Not Often, Never**)

1. encourage other people to have a turn to speak?   **A   O   S   N/O   N**

2. indicate in your gestures, facial expressions, or posture that you are interested in what is being said?   **A   O   S   N/O   N**

3. give people credit for their ideas and make them feel worthwhile, even if they disagree with you?   **A   O   S   N/O   N**

B. How difficult is it for you to...(**Extremely, Very, Somewhat, Difficult at Times, Not Difficult at All**)

1. encourage other people to have a turn to speak?   **E   V   S   D/T   N**

2. indicate in your gestures, facial expressions, or posture that you are interested in what is being said?   **E   V   S   D/T   N**

3. give people credit for their ideas and make them feel worthwhile, even if they disagree with you?   **E   V   S   D/T   N**

C. How successfully do you...(**Extremely, Very, Somewhat, Successfully at Times, Not Successfully**)

1. encourage other people to have a turn to speak?   **E   V   S   S/T   N**

2. indicate in your gestures, facial expressions, or posture that you are interested in what is being said?   **E   V   S   S/T   N**

3. give people credit for their ideas and make them feel worthwhile, even if they disagree with you?   **E   V   S   S/T   N**

Highlighted skill: evaluating in a group

Name _____ Class _____

Please consider your usual performance in a small-group discussion.

Highlighted Skill: **Evaluating in a Group** (Please circle your choice.)

A. How often do you...(**Always, Often, Sometimes, Not Often, Never**)

1. indicate whether or not you agree with ideas or
   decisions and why you do or don't ?   **A   O   S   N/O   N**

2. consider how well the group is working and how
   you might help the group work even better?   **A   O   S   N/O   N**

3. re-examine your own opinions and decisions and
   adjust them when someone comes up with a
   better idea?   **A   O   S   N/O   N**

B. How difficult is it for you to...(**Extremely, Very, Somewhat, Difficult
at Times, Not Difficult at All**)

1. indicate whether or not you agree with ideas or
   decisions and why you do or don't ?   **E   V   S   D/T   N**

2. consider how well the group is working and how
   you might help the group work even better?   **E   V   S   D/T   N**

3. re-examine your own opinions and decisions and
   adjust them when someone comes up with a
   better idea?   **E   V   S   D/T   N**

C. How successfully do you...(**Extremely, Very, Somewhat,
Successfully at Times, Not Successfully**)

1. indicate whether or not you agree with ideas or
   decisions and why you do or don't ?   **E   V   S   S/T   N**

2. consider how well the group is working and how
   you might help the group work even better?   **E   V   S   S/T   N**

3. re-examine your own opinions and decisions and
   adjust them when someone comes up with a
   better idea?   **E   V   S   S/T   N**

5 * Evaluating personal response

As much as educators emphasize the intrinsic goals of learning, extrinsic forces, in particular, marks, fuel the learning/teaching environment. This chapter will explain in detail why and how response journals are marked, especially for report card purposes. Students ask:

"Does this count for report cards?"

"How is it going to be marked? What's it worth?"

Teachers ask:

"How do we make this kind of work count for report card purposes?"

"How do you mark it? What should it be worth?"

From the junior grades on, students become increasingly aware that marks are a very important indicator of how their teachers and their parents value their efforts. Like it or not, calls for accountability in education always have a disturbing side effect. Marks take on even more importance to everyone involved, including the students.

Sample response to traditional evaluation (tests)

Traditionally, evaluation has denoted test-taking or examinations. During these tests, students prove how much they've learned by answering questions devised by their teachers. The intent is to help students review and solidify their learning. The results, on the other hand, denote the level of achievement to teacher, parent, and student alike. When the test or exam, in effect, becomes the learning criterion, the format often overwhelms and obscures the intent. Test-makers and test-takers assume adversarial roles, as this next student response dramatically illustrates. An excellent student, Li Li is caught up in a frustrating, anxiety-riddled process that has little to do with learning and that, unfortunately, is all too common.

Response to tests

"Tests." Whenever people referred to this word, I would feel uncomfortable and start to hate. A pile of stuff I have to memorize, a bunch of notes I have to read, and a stack of hard words I have to know how to spell. In the next few weeks, tests are coming in French, math, science, shop, and geography. Oh, no. I will die with these piles and piles of tests. To be a good student is extremely hard.

These things made me crazy, I suddenly realized. I felt fussy. I felt tired. "No more school!" I recalled those words. I really wanted to cry, but I controlled my tears. I don't know what to do with these bunches of tests. But, of course, I did know. Read your notes and memorize them. But I felt a large piece of emptiness in my head. I can't remember a lot of notes. Of course I've tried before and it's been no use. I really can't remember anything. My brain seemed suddenly converted to stupid. Just like a small five-year-old kid, I didn't know anything. I frowned. I punched the pillow. I even threw the pots on the floor. But no matter what I did, the stupid brain could not remember the notes.

> *"Settle down, settle down," I murmured to myself. I sat in silence for a while. I took out the notes and read them slowly. Very slowly. Turn the notes over and try to remember them. Finally, very slowly, I was able to write down the notes without looking at them. I knew I would get it. I felt really proud of myself, really proud. But the hate of tests still stays in my heart.*
>
> *Li Li W. (age 12)*

Fortunately, if evaluation is truly integrated with the learning process, summative evaluation can actually drive that process in a powerful and positive way.

If teachers are able to identify their objectives, articulate what students have to do to reach those objectives, and reward them accordingly for doing so, then summative evaluation becomes integral to the learning. The essential elements in the evaluation of response journals involve identifying appropriate learning objectives and rewarding process as well as product.

Formative and summative evaluation

Perhaps this is the place to say a few words about formative and summative evaluation. (See also **evaluation** in the glossary.) Formative evaluation is the ongoing assessment of student progress aimed almost exclusively at assisting students in their learning and at improving the educational experience. Such evaluation is geared to an individual's needs and personal growth.

Summative evaluation, however, usually employs comparative standards and judgments in order to make an overall decision (e.g., any assessment made and recorded for report card purposes). Most people assume that formative evaluation is a means to an end and that summative evaluation is an end in itself. If that were the case, summative evaluation would always be counter-productive to the learning process because it happens after the learning. Marks achieved in the final summative evaluation would signify the amount of learning accomplished, and so students would focus on getting better marks rather than on learning *per se*. For this reason, teachers must use summative evaluation in a way that turns student attention back to the learning experience instead of merely fixating it on the test itself. In fact, if applied appropriately, summative evaluation can have an important formative outcome.

Many theorists point to formative evaluation as the focal point in the learning process; classroom teachers recognize that importance, but realize how truncated the formative process usually turns out to be. Many teachers for example, have only eight weeks from the time they first meet a group of students to the time they write their first set of comprehensive report cards. Students learn early how the system operates. Theorists tell classroom teachers that self-evaluation is the ultimate goal of education; teachers reply that the first question their students ask is, "Does this count on my report card?"

The key to turning summative evaluation into a powerful, positive force for learning lies in declaring and defining clear objectives — right up front for everyone to see, especially the students. If students know precisely the criteria by which they will be evaluated, they will more readily direct their efforts to meeting those criteria; if, in fact, students have the opportunity to set some of those criteria themselves, they can actually take over responsibility for their learning.

Do you mark surface errors?

As teachers begin to incorporate response journals into their programs, they are unsure about what to do with the spelling mistakes and grammatical errors found in the journals. Since they've heard the cry for so long that "every teacher is an English teacher", they assume the concept compels them to identify and have their students correct all the surface errors they discover in the journals. Nothing could be further from the truth.

A student's personal language is essential to the learning process. As students pick away at and think through assorted facts, impressions, memories, and feelings, their use of language is often hesitant, tentative, halting, repetitive, and recursive. The language itself is informal, natural, and spontaneous. When students write in their journals in this mode, surface errors are common. The primary goal is learning and surface errors do not impede the learning process. If the goal were communication with others, then students would have to take a more rigorous approach to the writing process. They would draft, revise, edit, proofread, and eventually, make the writing public. But a personal response is very definitely *not* a formal essay.

If surface features or modes of expression in journals were marked, the outpouring of thoughts and feelings would be impeded and students would be much more reluctant to take risks. What they were attempting to understand would become secondary to whether or not a particular word was spelled correctly. The spontaneous flow of language and thought would be effectively destroyed. Since response journals direct students to examine the crucial link between how and what they learn, evaluation must be based on *learning* criteria rather than on *fluency* criteria. If a teacher is having difficulty deciphering a student's handwriting, the teacher can still sit down with that student, point out the problem, and decide how best to resolve it. On the other hand, surface errors should never be marked and should never be weighted in the evaluation system.

No surprises

Right from the start, students have to be included in the total process of using response journals. They need to know what they are, why and how they will be used, and most importantly, how they will be evaluated. Their own suggestions for implementing and operating the journals should be considered. If possible, the group and/or individuals might suggest or select some of the evaluation criteria.

Whatever teachers want to happen in those journals should be clearly articulated and those criteria should be built into the evaluation system. If the objectives are clearly stated, evaluation can direct and support the learning process. For example, if teachers feel that students should be looking back at past entries and reflecting on their own growth or changes in their opinions, they should tell them in advance that their journals need to include this kind of item. They should show them the marking scheme they'll be using and indicate how long it will be before they formally evaluate their work.

Over a two- or three-week period, check informally or with self-evaluation checklists to see if students are, in fact, including that kind of entry in their journals and discuss with them how they view their progress (formative evaluation). After the designated period of time, assign a mark for the extent to which each student has met that criterion (summative evaluation). By discussing with a student how the mark was arrived at and what the student would have to do to improve the mark over the next evaluation period, teachers can make the mark work for them in a formative manner.

Variations are possible. If teachers want to emphasize one specific criterion, they can simply weight it with more marks. As students become more adept at certain kinds of entries, teachers may want to stimulate other uses by changing the marking emphasis. In collaboration with their students before each evaluation period, they can decide which criteria to retain and which to discard. They can even individualize the marking scheme for certain students to stimulate a specific aspect of growth. One of the most important features of response journals is that they supply concrete evidence of a process over time. To stimulate process objectives, teachers need to include process as well as product criteria in their evaluation schemes.

Sample summative evaluation criteria

The following criteria for summative evaluation reflect the wide potential of response journals. Given the range of subject areas and integrative situations possible, however, this generic list is not meant to be exhaustive. At the same time, such criteria can apply in a variety of learning/teaching contexts. Although the structural context may change, the specific learning objectives do not. The criteria a teacher uses should reflect his or her specific program objectives over a specific period of time. For example, asking for three extended responses over a five-day cycle is a purely arbitrary measure. Teachers need to adjust requirements to reflect their students' skills and needs and their particular learning/teaching situation. Still, these criteria can be used effectively as initial general guidelines.

To what extent do the entries indicate that the student has:

- kept a complete record of such experiences as research or reference books read, excursions, hands-on activities, films, special presentations, small-group discussions (list topic and group members), teacher-directed responses, specific lessons?

- responded to at least some of the experiences offered per cycle (or week) in an extended manner?

- responded in a sincere, thoughtful, and reflective manner (entries display evidence of personal involvement, analysis, and syntheses)?

- kept track of his/her role in group discussions, reviewed past performances, and attempted to strengthen specific skills?

- recorded questions/comments/observations for later reference (e.g., for student-teacher conference or for an independent study unit)?

- looked back at previous entries and attempted to reflect on the experiences, opinions, emotions expressed in them?

Notice how well those criteria fit all of the following learning/teaching contexts:

- a specific theme (e.g., "The Depression Years")

- one term of a subject-specific course (e.g., science)

- a multidisciplinary unit (e.g., English/history/geography)

- an interdisciplinary course (e.g., myths)

For an independent study component of any course, the criteria could be augmented with such items as the following:
    To what extent do the entries indicate that the student has:

- kept a complete record of all books read and references consulted?

- included a variety of personal responses to reading selections?

- kept a complete record of media experiences and articulated personal responses to each?

- kept track of student-teacher conferences, comments made, and specific goals set?

Sample summative evaluation instruments

A variety of evaluation instruments can be devised based on identified criteria. A few such summative — and formative — instruments are included below. In all summative evaluations, although only the teacher mark is counted for report card purposes, a student mark should also be required. If it isn't included, why require student input at all?
    Self-evaluation is a complex and difficult skill that develops over a long period of time. Through applying various evaluation criteria to their own efforts, students begin to internalize those criteria, a vital step on the road to developing mature, self-evaluative skills. If the teacher and student differ significantly in their appraisals of the work, that difference can serve as the basis for a fruitful student-

teacher conference. As well, even though the student mark is not directly counted, the student can establish a case for a series of responses and direct the teacher to the material's outstanding features.

Tailoring the summative instruments

The first sample instrument on page 81 demonstrates how to include all of the criteria discussed so far for measuring the effectiveness of the response journal in a single summative marks sheet. Notice how the second and third criteria are weighted to ensure attention.

For a particular period, however, a teacher may want to narrow the focus in order to stimulate a specific aspect of the program. An adjusted marks sheet is supplied on page 82 to reflect *selected* criteria. Fewer criteria are included and the weighting is adjusted accordingly.

Another option is to include student input in the criteria. How much teachers do in this regard or when they start will depend on an individual class and the students' stages of readiness. But if teachers want students to become involved in the program as quickly and completely as possible, they should consider including them in the process of devising evaluation criteria for marks. They can ease into this process in several ways.

• Brainstorm a list of criteria with the students. Through discussion, prioritize and short-list the items.

• To individualize the marking scheme, reserve a certain amount (perhaps 25%) for items not chosen by the teacher. Each student is then asked to add items worth that amount to an individual marking scheme.

The sample marks sheet on page 83 shows how the teacher and student can *share* in the selection of criteria to be used in the teacher's evaluation for summative purposes.

In an **interdisciplinary** unit, the criteria will grow out of the objectives of the course. The journal can easily be marked with an instrument similar to the marks sheet for stated criteria on page 81.

In a **multidisciplinary** unit, the teachers involved decide beforehand what criteria are essential and blend those criteria into one marks sheet, again similar to the marks sheet for stated criteria on page 81.

Marking response journals: summative evaluation

Summative Evaluation Based on Explicitly Stated Criteria

Name: _____ Class: _____

Evaluation Period: from _____ to _____

To what extent do the entries indicate that the student has:

(S = student, T = teacher)

	S	T
• kept complete records as directed?	S /5	T /5
• responded to at least three (or two, or four) of the directed experiences per cycle in an extended manner?	S /10	T /10
• responded in a sincere, thoughtful, and reflective manner (personal connections explored and analyzed)?	S /15	T /15
• described role in small-group discussions thoughtfully?	S /5	T /5
• in small-group discussions, reviewed past discussions and attempts to improve skills?	S /5	T /5
• recorded questions/comments/observations for later reference and use?	S /5	T /5
• looked back at, reflected on, and tried to build on previous entries?	S /5	T /5
Totals:	S ☐/50	T ☐/50

Student Comment:

_____

_____

_____

Teacher Comment:

_____

_____

_____

Summative Evaluation Based on Selected Criteria

Name: _____ Class: _____

Evaluation Period: from _____ to _____

To what extent do the entries indicate that the student has:

(S = student, T = teacher)

• kept complete records as directed?   S /5   T /5

• responded to at least three of the directed
experiences per cycle in an extended
manner?   S /10   T /10

• responded in a sincere, thoughtful, and
reflective manner (personal connections
explored and analyzed)?   S /20   T /20

• described role in small-group discussions
thoughtfully?   S /5   T /5

• in small-group discussions, reviewed past
discussions and attempted to improve
skills?   S /10   T /10

                            Totals: S ☐/50   T ☐/50

Student Comment:

_____

_____

_____

Teacher Comment:

_____

_____

_____

Summative Evaluation Based on Shared Criteria

Name: _____ Class: _____

Evaluation Period: from _____ to _____

To what extent do the entries indicate that the student has:

(S = student, T = teacher)

Teacher-chosen criteria

- kept complete records as directed?   S /5   T /5

- responded to at least three of the directed
  experiences per cycle in an extended
  manner?   S /10   T /10

- responded in a sincere, thoughtful, and
  reflective manner (personal connections
  explored and analyzed)?   S /15   T /15

Student-chosen criteria

- read and responded in detail to a related
  book?   S /10   T /10

- collaborated well with other students and
  teacher?   S /10   T /10

                              Totals: S □/50   T □/50

Student Comment:

_____

_____

_____

Teacher Comment:

_____

_____

_____

Formative evaluation

Teachers usually mark response journals, for summative purposes, about twice a term. The process is straightforward. The students read over their entries for the designated evaluation period, fill out the evaluation sheet, and hand the journal in. The teacher then reads and marks the journal as well. A significant difference of any kind between the student and teacher conclusions provides a basis for discussion, negotiation, and further clarification and understanding of the learning criteria.

Formative evaluation, on the other hand, takes a variety of forms and occurs more frequently. Once the journal routines are established, many teachers like to read four or five journals a day. The practice takes only fifteen or twenty minutes. Within seven days or less, the teacher can become acquainted with how the class is coping with the response process. The cycle can then begin again. After a certain point, when the teacher is confident that all students are comfortable with the criteria and how to meet them, the journals can be handed in on a voluntary basis. At any time, when a student wants specific feedback from the teacher, he or she hands in the journal.

Formative evaluation routines

As noted earlier, to reinforce the students' sense of ownership of the process and the journals themselves, many teachers respond to journal entries on "stick-on" message paper or a separate sheet of paper. Time and again, students have indicated how much they appreciate it when teachers do not write directly on their entries. Even this small gesture makes a significant statement about how teachers value their students' efforts. The students can also decide whether or not to retain the communication. Some students leave the teacher responses where they were placed, some save them at the back of their journals, and others discard them. The teacher can discreetly initial the page in the journal at which he or she stopped reading on each marking occasion and begin at that initialled point the next time the journal is handed in.

(See also the formative suggestions and questionnaires for developing small-group discussion skills in Chapter 4, **Integrating co-operative learning**, pages 58 to 72.)

When they reply to a series of journal entries, teachers might comment on the frequency, depth, or variety of the responses. They might choose to respond to a single, especially stimulating or provocative entry. They might even choose to model the process by responding to something found in an entry in a personally significant manner.

To be effective, the teacher comment need not be lengthy, only sincere and specific to what each student has written. The traditional "good work" or "well done", while well-meaning, tend to militate against the principles of personal response. Students may take such responses as perfunctory and begin to reply in kind. They need to be reassured that the singular viewpoints they are attempting to develop are truly recognized.

These formative evaluations should be thought of not as marks but as an ongoing dialogue. Marking — or summative evaluation — should take place *after* the learning/teaching, not during.

Formative self-evaluation

At regular intervals, teachers should ask their students to step back and evaluate their own responses on the basis of the outlined objectives. Students can review their own progress, assess the extent to which they are meeting the objectives, and set new goals for themselves.

If students are to assume an active role in the learning process, they need to see evaluation as a tool and to feel they have some control over its use. They need to understand how evaluation can help them and they need to practice self-evaluation on a regular basis. As they gain in confidence and skill, more mature students will often be able to apply their own criteria in their own way and for their own purposes.

In most cases, however, teachers will need to consciously promote opportunities for their students to practice self-evaluation. Depending on the needs of the group, a teacher may want to include a more formal "taking stock" component as part of the formative evaluation process. Students can be directed to read over and reflect on their responses in a comprehensive way. In this manner they become aware themselves how well they are meeting the various evaluative criteria and can use the exercise as a dress rehearsal for a summative evaluation to come. While demanding and detailed, the instrument overleaf demonstrates one way in which this more formal formative evaluation could be conducted.

Marking response journals: formative self-evaluation

Formative Self-Evaluation

Student directions:

Please read your journal entries for the period from _____ to _____.

To what extent are you meeting the expectations of the personal response component and specific outcomes established for the journal? How can you improve your responses before the next evaluation date?

As you consider these questions and begin framing your response in your journal, you should consider these additional questions. While you don't need to answer each one, you should use them as a guideline for how detailed your response should be.

Please respond in your journals.

• How complete is your tracking? What gaps are you leaving? Why?

• How many extended responses have you made in this period? How many should you have to meet the minimum standards (two or three per cycle)?

• How varied are your responses? To what extent do you respond to only a few kinds of experiences? What kind of entries, if any, have you been neglecting?

• How thoughtful, searching, inquisitive, probing, and involved are your entries? To what extent is it evident that you are attempting to make sense of the course and the experiences you meet? To what extent are you attempting to fit the experiences of the course into your own real-life experiences?

• If you were the teacher evaluating this journal, what impressions would you form of the person making these entries and the extent to which he or she is sincerely and actively trying to make the most of a variety of learning experiences?

Sample student response to formative self-evaluation

When students have the opportunity to self-evaluate, they often respond in surprising ways. When sincere, however, the input can have significant impact, regardless of how unexpected it might be. Before replying to the following student journal entry, the teacher would also have to go through a reflective and self-evaluative process. Part of this process and the teacher's subsequent reply follow the student entry.

I think I'm going to lose marks because I haven't kept up with my tracking. It's really hard to remember how to do that all the time. Besides, you could be so busy keeping track of everything that you wouldn't have time to do all the extended responses that you have to do. What's the use of writing down all the discussions we have and everything else that we do if we're not going to do extended responses to them. I think it just wastes time.

I noticed that I'm getting better at discussions. I used to talk a lot more than I do now and I've been asking a lot of questions in the group. I like responding to films most of all because you can say whatever is on your mind and not worry about whether or not you're right or about a test. Like if you were sitting around and talking about it with your friends only most of the films you see in school aren't as good as real films except maybe ones like that pollution film or the advertising film. My all-time favourite was "Killing Us Softly." It was weird to look at ads after that and see all the sexist stuff you never saw before.

I think I understand everything really well and except for the tracking, I think I'll get pretty good on my journal.

Paul C. (age 13)

Sample teacher reply to student self-evaluation

When a teacher reads a response, the act of formulating a reply merges with a rapid, almost subliminal inner dialogue. Everything the teacher knows about the student, the program, and how the two are interrelating comes into question. If this inner dialogue as a result of reading Paul's response could be transcribed, a portion might look like this:

> *Is the criticism of the tracking component justified? How laborious and tedious is the task of tracking? Of what value is it? How objective has Paul been about the features he's described and the progress he's made? What has he left out and why? What specific aspects of his journal are praiseworthy? What concrete suggestions would lead to improvement? How much criticism, regardless of how constructive it is, can Paul accept without becoming discouraged? What kind of tone would make the reply and the criticism palatable?*

The teacher might reply in an informal conference with the student or in writing. Regardless of the form, this kind of comprehensive self-evaluation by the student deserves an equally comprehensive teacher response.

If the purpose of evaluation were to collect marks in order to slot, sort out, or compare students, the process would demean both student and teacher and belittle, obscure, and distort learning. With response journals, evaluation should stem from and support the learning criteria. The time taken to frame a thoughtful reply to a thoughtful response is well spent. In this case, the teacher tries to fold constructive criticism into a deliberately structured, carefully complimentary response.

Thank you, Paul, for such a detailed and extended self-evaluation. I certainly agree with you about the skills you're developing in discussion groups. I've noticed how you've been trying to help everyone participate. One reason to track the topic under discussion and include the names of the group members is to help you look back and see how effectively you work with various people, what the differences might be, and what you might be able to do about those differences. Seeing the topic and who you were working with might also be enough to trigger your recollection of what you talked about.

I think I can be more consistent about making sure that everyone has a few moments at the end of each period to take care of any tracking that needs to be done. That way, you should have the time you need. Since your journal is a portfolio of your work in this class and a record of what you've actually done, I think it's important to keep accurate and complete records.

I did notice that you haven't kept up with the minimum number of extended responses required. By responding each day for the next two weeks, you should be able to catch up nicely. You may want to take your journal home and work on it there. Since you haven't responded to an actual lesson in a while, why not make that one of your priorities?

By the way, I've always enjoyed your reactions to films. You make relevant and spontaneous comments and often develop fresh and intriguing perspectives on the issues involved. I'm looking forward to reading and learning from the responses you develop over the next little while.

Mr. P.

Afterword

If our goal is to develop life-long learners, we need to become committed to the processes that produce independence in learning. Life-long learners feel positive about learning, take responsibility for their own learning; and they have learned how to learn. They need to be self-motivated and self-directed problem-finders and problem-solvers. They need to understand not only the processes of inquiry, analysis, synthesis, and evaluation, but also how they, as individuals, go about those processes. Life-long learners need to see themselves as perceptive, resourceful, intuitive, and creative.

Like it or not, with or without us, our students are always learning. The only question, really, is whether we join them or try to force them to join us. In the latter case, we become more like horse trainers than teachers, using bridle, bit, and blinkers to force students onto a track of our choosing to pursue goals of our making. By truly collaborating, on the other hand, we help them refine and extend skills they already possess, process and expand the experiences that intrigue them, and identify and resolve the conflicts that confound them. As facilitators and guides, we help them explore the fascinations of their own lives and, from that foundation, grow naturally to face the challenges of the wider world.

When next we begin to plan the outcomes for a group of students, or devise a test to evaluate their achievement, or stand at the front of our classrooms prior to teaching a lesson, we need to remember that students already have the power of language, of personal response, and of learning. It we're wise, we will give them the opportunity to share their learning with us. Perhaps, then, we can more often match what we're teaching to what they need and want to learn. To become more effective as teachers, we need to ask our students, particularly those who feel like the author of the following poem, to let us see them and ourselves more clearly through their eyes.

Students like Anne need to enter into a sincere dialogue with a sensitive, caring teacher. The fact that she wrote this poem indicates that she is struggling with an idea of school and of herself.

You

All this talk about symbolism bores you.
You sit at the back of the class,
With your hair hanging in your face,
Eyes half-closed.
Or are they?
Feet stretched out under the seat in front of you,
Chin touched to your chest,
Fingers linked together.
You stand out from all the rest.
They are all sitting up straight,
Pens ceaselessly moving,
Copying down the teacher's every word.
Full attention to the front of the class,
When mine's to the back,
Not obvious, or so I try to make it,
Studying your every move.
Not much to study.
Thinking how alike I am to them.
The bell rings.
You're the first one up, and out of the room,
Like it is your mating call.

Anne K. (age 14)

Personal response helps with such struggles. Through language we are able to make sense of and to cope with our world and, eventually, to sort out and make sense of ourselves. Through personal response, students are given the power to explore their inner worlds, their outer worlds, and the myriad connections between. Personal response liberates students and sets them on the path to life-long learning. Personal response is empowering.

Index of responses

The student responses found throughout this book can also be used as models of what is possible or appropriate for your students. If individuals or groups are having difficulty deepening, broadening, or varying their responses, teachers should consider sharing some of these responses with them. The responses are listed in the same order as they are found in the book.

Response to:

Glossary

The definitions in this selected glossary reflect the meanings that are used in the text.

affective: a term from psychology referring to emotional activity.

behaviorist: focussing on observable behavior; also arranging learning experiences in scope and sequence and applying rewards and reviews to help students make successful, step-by-step progress.

brainstorming: generating a list of examples, ideas, or questions to illustrate, expand, or explore a central idea or topic (record all ideas; no evaluating of ideas during collecting; quantity of ideas is important; encourage students to expand on each other's ideas; "zany" ideas are welcome).

cognitive: a term from psychology referring to intellectual activity.

co-operative learning: a variety of small-group, instructional techniques focussing on peer collaboration.

cueing response: making a guiding suggestion or hint that gives an individual a sense of the kinds of responses possible. The cues serve as examples or models, but individuals are encouraged to develop their own responses based on their own purposes for learning and their personal perspectives as independent learners.

curriculum: at one time, a synonym for syllabus; the current definition reflects the complexity of learning; in effect, it refers to everything that happens in a school.

diary (private): an in-class record of personal observations, random jottings, daily record of thoughts and feelings; shared only if the student agrees; difficult to maintain over time or adapt for use in other parts of the writing program (see also **journal**).

evaluation: determining progress toward and attainment of specific goals; assessing progress and achievement and program effectiveness (See also **diagnostic, formative**, and **summative**, below).

> **diagnostic:** a type of formative evaluation; becoming familiar with each student's interests, abilities, preferred learning style, and learning difficulties.

> **formative:** the ongoing assessment of student progress aimed almost exclusively at assisting learning and at improving the educational experience; geared to an individual's needs and personal growth.

> **summative:** usually employs comparative standards and judgments in order to make an overall conclusion (e.g., any assessment made and recorded for report card purposes).

fluency: the ability to speak, write, or read aloud smoothly, easily, and with clear expression of ideas.

hemisphericity: the concept that the left and right hemispheres of the brain have different capacities and functions; educators commonly speak of right- and left-brain dominance, believing, for example, that the left brain controls speech and most language functions, while the right brain controls visual and spatial skills; theorizing that children may possess a dominant hemisphere, many educators advocate identifying it and teaching to it.

integrated studies: the combining of separate parts or components into a functioning whole — e.g., teachers collaborating to focus on similar content or skills or separate disciplines combined into one.

interdisciplinary: describes the merging of separate subject areas — e.g., history and geography.

journal (public): a less private form of diary; is more readily shared, serves more functions, and is more adaptable as a teaching tool; especially useful when used to elicit personal responses to reading and issues and events under study and treated as exploratory, a part of the writing process.

learning through language: also referred to as "language across the curriculum", an approach to the learning/teaching environment that recognizes that language is intrinsic to thinking and learning; among the basic principles is the realization that students need to "think aloud" in their own talk or style of writing in order to fully understand concepts; during the talking and writing process, concepts are examined, analyzed, reformulated, and defined in a personal and individual manner.

literacy: the ability to read and write; extended today to include the processing of information from all sources and systems, including electronic and microelectronic.

making meaning: a term that recognizes that the act of processing language involves more than the passive recording of experience; through language we tend to construct our sense of things by clarifying, discovering, assessing, reflecting on, resolving, and refining what we really think and feel about experience.

metacognition: the study of thought processes.

multidisciplinary: describes two or more subject areas focussing on the same content or group of skills.

personal response: an explication of and reflection on material with one's own idiosyncratic, immediate, and spontaneous impressions, reactions, and questions where and when they arise.

psychomotor: a term from psychology referring to physical activity.

response journal: a notebook or folder in which students record their personal reactions to, questions about, and reflections on what they read, write, view, listen to, do, and discuss in addition to how they actually go about reading, writing, viewing, listening, doing, and discussing.

risk-taking: experimenting, extending the known, or trying something new without unduly worrying about failing or being wrong.

transactional: a mode of teaching in which "doing" is an integral component; often "hands-on", in the sense of experimentation; the scientific method.

transformational: a mode of teaching that focusses on developing reflection in the learner and internal change; metacognition is essential.

transmission: a mode of teaching in which information is passed from teacher to student in lecture form; basically "telling".

webbing: a commonly used method of graphically linking and organizing associated concepts, thoughts, symbols, and related activities.

whole language: a learning/teaching approach that emphasizes the integration of language "threads" (i.e., listening, speaking, reading, writing, thinking) within the context of meaningful communication (e.g., a single writing task may engage a student in a range of discussion, composing, editing/revising, reading tasks); includes the idea of moving away from isolated, fragmented approaches such as a regular "grammar" period outside the context of the writing process.

writing modes: identified as expressive, poetic, and transactional; all modes can be accommodated within the response journal format.

   expressive: includes such forms as sharing personal experiences, personal response writing, exploratory writing, projecting oneself into the experience of another, personal letters.

   poetic: includes vivid stories and metaphorical use of language in poems, patterning from literature.

   transactional: focusses on providing information; includes reports, instructions, arguments, scientific observations, business letters.

Selected and annotated bibliography

The following references emerged as touchstones as this book developed. Some of the references are timeless, their messages to educators as vivid and as relevant now as anything written today. Others are brand-new voices, offering much-needed advice and a fresh perspective. The list is decidedly idiosyncratic and notable for the many fine texts not mentioned.

Atwell, Nancie. *In the Middle: Writing, Reading, and Learning with Adolescents*. Portsmouth, New Hampshire: Boynton/Cook Publishers, 1987. (One teacher's personal narrative of how she worked her way through to a better understanding of how to help her students "make meaning"; presents a real teacher with real students in a real classroom.)

Barnes, Douglas. *From Communication to Curriculum*. Harmondsworth: Penguin, 1976. (Establishes and explores the fundamental principles of language use in classrooms; as stimulating now as when first published.)

Beane, James A. "Creating an Integrative Curriculum: Making the Connections". NASSP Bulletin, v76 n547, November 1992. (A profound and stimulating challenge to the traditional way of looking at an integrated curriculum; goes beyond tinkering with structure to a re-examination of what curriculum should be.)

Caine, Renate Nummela, and Geoffrey Caine. *Making Connections: Teaching and the Human Brain*. Virginia: Association for Supervision and Curriculum Development, 1993. (An objective, comprehensive examination of the neurosciences and a direct extrapolation of the findings to education; explodes a number of current myths in education, including the "love affair" with hemisphericity.)

Fullan, Michael, and Andy Hargreaves. *What's Worth Fighting For? Working Together for Your Schools*. Toronto, Ontario: Ontario Public School Teachers' Federation, 1991. (A seminal and persuasive account of a collaborative curriculum. The authors decide that everything in schools is negotiable, including whole language and co-operative learning; even if you don't agree with them, you're forced to articulate for yourself "what's worth fighting for".)

Graves, Donald H. *Discover Your Own Literacy*. Portsmouth, New Hampshire: Heinemann, 1990. (A vision of the classroom as a community of learners within which adults and children together investigate and develop their own literacy.)

Parsons, Les. *Response Journals*. Markham, Ontario: Pembroke Publishers Limited/Portsmouth, New Hampshire: Heinemann Educational Books, Inc., 1990. (A comprehensive, pragmatic system for implementing a whole-language program based on personal response.)

Spear, Karen. *Sharing Writing: Peer Response Groups in English Classes*. Portsmouth, New Hampshire: Boynton/Cook Publishers, 1988. (Highlights the use of peer response in writing classes. The principles apply directly to co-operative discussion groups.)

Thomson, Jack. *Understanding Teenagers' Reading: Reading Processes and the Teaching of Literature*. New York: Nichols Publishing Co., 1987. (Places personal response in a historical context and establishes the theoretical and research foundation for personal response approaches.)

Vars, Gordon F. *Interdisciplinary Teaching in the Middle Grades*. Columbus, Ohio: National Middle School Association, 1992. (The structures developed to explain and deal with interdisciplinary teaching are many, varied, and, increasingly, obscure; this clear-cut, practical treatment outlines the why's and how's in a no-nonsense manner.)